LITERATURE MADE EASY

WILLIAM SHAKESPEARE'S

JULIUS CAESAR

Written by RUTH COLEMAN
WITH TONY BUZAN

BARRON'S

First edition for the United States and Canada published by Barron's Educational Series, Inc., 1999.

First published in the United Kingdom by Hodder & Stoughton Ltd. under the title: *Teach Yourself Literature Guides: A Guide to Julius Caesar*

Cover photograph © The Ronald Grant Archive
Mind Maps: David Orr
Illustrations: Karen Donnelly

American text edited by Elizabeth Schmid

All inquiries should be addressed to:
Barron's Educational Series, Inc.
250 Wireless Boulevard
Hauppauge, New York 11788
http://www.barronseduc.com

International Standard Book No. 0-7641-0833-6
Library of Congress Catalog Card No. 98-73260

PRINTED IN THE UNITED STATES OF AMERICA
9 8 7 6 5 4 3 2 1

CONTENTS

There are five important things you must know about your brain and memory to revolutionize
the way you study:

◆ how your memory
  ("recall") works *while* you are learning
◆ how your memory works *after* you have finished learning
◆ how to use Mind Maps – a special technique for helping you
  with all aspects of your studies
◆ how to prepare for tests and exams.

Recall during learning
– THE NEED FOR BREAKS

When you are studying, your memory
can concentrate, understand, and
remember well for between 20 and 45
minutes at a time; then it needs a
break. If you carry on for longer than
this without a break, your memory
starts to break down. If you study for
hours nonstop, you will remember only a small fraction of what
you have been trying to learn, and you will have wasted hours
of valuable time.

So, ideally, *study for less than an hour*, then take a five- to ten-
minute break. During the break listen to music, go for a walk, do
some exercise, or just daydream. (Daydreaming is a necessary
brain-power booster – geniuses do it regularly.) During the break
your brain will be sorting out what it has been learning, and you
will go back to your books with the new information safely
stored and organized in your memory. We recommend breaks
at regular intervals as you work through this book. Make sure
you take them!

Recall after learning
– THE WAVES OF YOUR MEMORY

What do you think begins to happen to your
memory right after you have finished learning something?
Does it immediately start forgetting? No! Your brain actually
increases its power and continues remembering. For a short
time after your study session, your brain integrates the
information, making a more complete picture of everything it
has just learned. Only then does the rapid decline in memory
begin, and as much as 80 percent of what you have learned can
be forgotten in a day.

However, if you catch the top of the wave of your memory,
and briefly review (look back over) what you have been
studying at the correct time, the memory is imprinted far more
strongly, and stays at the crest of the wave for a much longer
time. To maximize your brain's power to remember, take a few
minutes at the end of a day and use a Mind Map to review
what you have learned. Then review it at the end of a week,
again at the end of a month, and finally a week before your
test or exam. That way you'll ride your memory
wave all the way there – and beyond!

The Mind Map ®
– A PICTURE OF THE WAY YOU THINK

Do you like taking notes? More important, do you like having to
go back over and learn them before tests or exams? Most
students I know certainly do not! And how do you take your
notes? Most people take notes on lined paper, using blue or
black ink. The result, visually, is boring. And what does *your*
brain do when it is bored? It turns off, tunes out, and goes to
sleep! Add a dash of color, rhythm, imagination, and the whole
note-taking process becomes much more fun, uses more of your
brain's abilities, and improves your recall and understanding.

Generally, your Mind Map is highly personal and need not be
understandable to any other person. It mirrors *your* brain. Its
purpose is to build up your "memory muscle" by creating
images that will help you recall instantly the most important

points about characters and plot sequences in a work of fiction you are studying.

You will find Mind Maps throughout this book. Study them, add some color, personalize them, and then try drawing your own – you'll remember them far better. Stick them in your files and on your walls for a quick-and-easy review of the topic.

HOW TO DRAW A MIND MAP

1 First of all, briefly examine the Mind Maps and Mini Mind Maps used in this book. What are the common characteristics? All of them use small pictures or symbols, with words branching our from the illustration.
2 Decide which idea or character in the book you want to illustrate and draw a picture, starting in the middle of the page so that you have plenty of room to branch out. Remember that no one expects a young Rembrandt or Picasso here; artistic ability is not as important as creating an image you (and you alone) will remember. A round smiling (or sad) face might work as well in your memory as a finished portrait. Use marking pens of different colors to make your Mind Map as vivid and memorable as possible.
3 As your thoughts flow freely, add descriptive words and other ideas on the colored branching lines that connect to the central image. Print clearly, using one word per line if possible.
4 Further refine your thinking by adding smaller branching lines, containing less important facts and ideas, to the main points.
5 Presto! You have a personal outline of your thoughts about the character and plot. It's not a stodgy formal outline, but a colorful image that will stick in your mind, it is hoped, throughout classroom discussions and final exams.

HOW TO READ A MIND MAP

1 Begin in the center, the focus of your topic.
2 The words/images attached to the center are like chapter headings; read them next.
3 Always read out from the center, in every direction (even on the left-hand side, where you will have to read from right to left, instead of the usual left to right).

USING MIND MAPS

Mind Maps are a versatile tool; use them for taking notes in class or from books, for solving problems, for brainstorming with friends, and for reviewing and working for tests or exams – their uses are endless. You will find them invaluable for planning essays for coursework and exams. Number your main branches in the order in which you want to use them and off you go – the main headings for your essay are done and all your ideas are logically organized.

Preparing for tests and exams

◆ Review your work systematically. Study hard at the beginning of your course, not the end, and avoid "exam panic."
◆ Use Mind Maps throughout your course, and build a Master Mind Map for each subject – a giant Mind Map that summarizes everything you know about the subject.
◆ Use memory techniques such as mnemonics (verses or systems for remembering such things as dates and events).
◆ Get together with one or two friends to study, compare Mind Maps, and discuss topics.

AND FINALLY...

Have *fun* while you learn – it has been shown that students who make their studies enjoyable understand and remember everything better and get the highest grades. I wish you and your brain every success! (Tony Buzan)

HOW TO USE THIS GUIDE

This guide assumes that you have already read *Julius Caesar*, although you could read Background and The Story of *Julius Caesar* before that. It is best to use the guide alongside the play. You could read the Who's Who? and Themes sections without referring to the play, but you will get more out of these sections if you do refer to it to check the points made, especially when thinking about the questions designed to test your recall and help you think about the play.

The Commentary section can be used in a number of ways. One way is to read a scene in the play, and then read the Commentary for that scene. Continue until you come to a test section, test yourself – and take a break. Or, read the Commentary for a scene, then read the scenes in the play, then go back to the Commentary. Find out what works best for you.

Topics for Discussion and Brainstorming gives topics that could well appear on exams or provide the basis for coursework. It would be particularly useful for you to discuss them with friends, or brainstorm them using Mind Map techniques (see p. vi).

How to Get an "A" in English Literature gives valuable advice on what to look for in any text, and what skills you need to develop to achieve a lifelong appreciation of literature.

The Exam Essay is a useful night-before reminder of how to tackle exam questions, and Model Answer and Essay Plans gives an example of an "A"-grade essay and the Mind Map and plan used to write it.

THE QUESTIONS

Whenever you come across a question in the guide with a star
✪ in front of it, think about it for a moment. You could even jot down a few words to focus your mind. There is not usually a "right" answer to these questions; it is important for you to develop your own opinions. The Test Yourself sections are

designed to take you about 10–20 minutes each – which will be time well spent. Take a short break after each one.

Important Note to Students About Line References

Line references are to The New Folger Library edition of Shakespeare's *Julius Caesar*. If you have another edition, the line numbers may vary slightly from those provided in this book, although the act and scene numbers should be the same. The line references from the New Folger edition have been provided to help direct you to specific parts of the play, but often will not be an exact match for line numbers in other editions.

Key to icons

THEMES

A **theme** is an idea explored by an author. Whenever a theme is dealt with in the guide, the appropriate icon is used. This means you can find a particular theme just by flicking through the book. Try it now.

Friendship
  and betrayal

Order
  and disorder

Nobility
  and honor

Ritual

Courage

Ill health

Fate
  and free will

 STYLE AND LANGUAGE

This heading and icon are used in the Commentary wherever there is a special section on the author's choice of words and imagery.

BACKGROUND

Did you know that the month of July was named after Julius Caesar? He added it to the calendar in 46 B.C. to create the unit of time we call a year. A great general, his stature as a man and demigod was so great that even over 2000 years after his death in 44 B.C. his influence touches our lives.

Shakespeare was fascinated by Julius Caesar and so were his battle-thirsty audiences. They knew the legend well and welcomed the opportunity to consider political issues that could be of topical relevance. The political stability of Elizabeth I's long reign was echoed in Caesar's dictatorship, and both types of government seemed to demonstrate that supreme rule by one person brought stability and order. There was little understanding of democracy, in which power is shared more equally between the people. Such regimes, favored by Brutus, were thought to be chaotic and undesirable. Shakespeare offers the audience an interpretation of what happens when an established order is challenged.

Source material for Julius Caesar

Shakespeare's source material for *Julius Caesar* was a translation of a work by the Greek philosopher and biographer, Plutarch, called *The Lives of the Noble Greeks and Romans*. Shakespeare maintains historical accuracy, but has sometimes changed the sequence and timing of events and embellished them with imaginative inventions of his own. Plutarch both praises and criticizes the actions of the main characters, and Shakespeare does the same. He offers us a thorough examination of this Roman conflict and invites us to make our own judgments.

Julius Caesar was completed in about 1599, the first of three "Roman plays." The second, *Antony and Cleopatra,* follows events in the life of Mark Antony after he takes power over Rome. Shakespeare wrote *Julius Caesar* after most of his history plays and before the great tragedies such as *Macbeth*, with which it has much in common. In *Julius Caesar*, Shakespeare mixes the dramatic styles of both history and tragedy.

POLITICS & COMMERCE

THE AGE OF

1580 - FRANCIS DRAKE BECAME FIRST ENGLISHMAN TO CIRCUMNAVIGATE THE WORLD

1586 - SIR WALTER RALEIGH IMPORTS TOBACCO FROM VIRGINIA

POTATO BROUGHT FROM COLOMBIA S.AMERICA

1587 - MARY QUEEN OF SCOTS (HALF SISTER OF ELIZABETH) EXECUTED AFTER FAILING TO RESTORE CATHOLICISM

QUEEN ELIZABETH I (1533-1603)

1588 - SPANISH ARMADA DEFEATED (129 SHIPS). ENGLAND DOMINATES THE SEAS

1605 - GUY FAWKES' GUNPOWDER PLOT TO BLOW UP HOUSES OF PARLIAMENT

1620 PILGRIM FATHERS BECOME FIRST ENGLISH SETTLERS IN NEW WORLD

THIS PERIOD IS ALSO KNOWN AS THE LATE RENAISSANCE, THE TERM USED TO DESCRIBE GREAT ADVANCEMENT OF KNOWLEDGE IN

SHAKESPEARE

ARTS AND SCIENCE

$a+b^2$

1579- DEVELOPMENTS IN ALGEBRA AND OTHER BRANCHES OF MATH

FIRST GLASS EYES MADE

1582- GREGORIAN CALENDER REPLACED WITH JULIAN IN EUROPE - USED EVER SINCE

1593- PLAYWRIGHT CHRISTOPHER MARLOWE KILLED IN TAVERN BRAWL

WILLIAM SHAKESPEARE (1564-1616)

1594 - TINTORETTO'S DEATH FOLLOWS THAT OF OTHER GREAT ARTISTS LEONARDO, MICHELANGELO, AND RAPHAEL

GALILEO (1564-1642) MAKES GREAT ADVANCES IN PHYSICS, MATH, AND ASTRONOMY. IDEAS UNPOPULAR WITH CHURCH

1597- IMPORTANT CHEMISTRY TEXTBOOK PUBLISHED (LIBAVIUS)

FIRST TELESCOPE (LIPPERSHEY)

SCIENCE, ART, NAVIGATION, AND COMMERCE. IT ENDED THE MIDDLE AGES AND BEGAN MODERN TIMES

1599 - FIRST SERIOUS WORK IN ZOOLOGY PUBUSHED (ALDROVANDI)

3

It is unusual to kill off the character after whom a work of literature is named as early as halfway through the work. By doing this Shakespeare divides the play into two stories.

The development of the conspiracy resulting in Caesar's assassination forms the first part; the second explores the power struggle that follows. The legend provided Shakespeare with the necessary ingredients for an examination of honor, nobility, and ambition, and friendship, betrayal, and revenge.

Empires and governments

? Take a few minutes to look at the picture summaries on either side of this page – they give you a flavor of the background to life for Shakespeare's audiences, and tell you a little about the Roman Empire. This will be time well spent because it will help you to understand the play. (Remember to start reading from the bottom up on p. 5 as all the dates are B.C.)

? What do you know about Caesar's Rome? Make a Mind Map.

? What do you understand by the words "dictator" and "democrat"? If you're not sure, look them up in a dictionary.

? Make a Mind Map of points for and against dictatorship and democracy.

now that you are familiar with Roman politics – on with the story

ROMAN EMPIRE

30 B.C. OCTAVIAN, LATER KNOWN AS AUGUSTUS, REIGNS SUPREME. END OF REPUBLIC.

31 B.C. BATTLE OF ACTIUM. ANTONY AND CLEOPATRA DEFEATED.

42 B.C. BATTLE OF PHILIPPI. BRUTUS AND CASSIUS KILLED.

43 B.C. SECOND TRIUMVIRATE (ANTONY, LEPIDUS, OCTAVIAN)

44 B.C. 15ᵗʰ MARCH, CAESAR MURDERED MARCH-MAY, MT. ETNA ERUPTS.

MAY-JUNE, COMET VISIBLE BY DAY ROMANS BELIEVE IT IS SPIRIT OF CAESAR — NOW A GOD.

45 B.C. CAESAR GIVEN CONSULSHIP FOR 10 YEARS, CONTROLS ENTRY TO SENATE, HAS SOLE COMMAND OF ARMED FORCES, AND IS MADE PERMANENT DICTATOR. AT THIS TIME, ROME STILL REPUBLIC BUT CONTROLLED BY ARISTOCRACY. CAESAR HAS SECRET AMBITION TO CREATE MONARCHY AND BECOME KING.

46 B.C. CAESAR CHANGES CALENDAR. NEW JULIAN CALENDAR HAS 3 YEARS OF 365 DAYS FOLLOWED BY 1 OF 366 DAYS. 46 B.C. HAD 455 DAYS TO CORRECT THE SEASONS, MAKING IT THE LONGEST ON RECORD.

49-48 B.C. CIVIL WAR BETWEEN CAESAR AND POMPEY, WHO HAD BIGGER ARMY & BETTER POSITION. BATTLE OF PHARSALUS & DEATH OF POMPEY. CAESAR COPES WITH PROBLEMS AT HOME AND CONDUCTS MILITARY CAMPAIGNS.

50-41 B.C. ROMAN ARCHITECT VITRUVIUS PUBLISHES BOOK. IT IS MAIN SOURCE OF KNOWLEDGE ABOUT CONSTRUCTION UNTIL RENAISSANCE.
54 & 55 B.C. CAESAR'S FIRST & SECOND INVASION OF BRITAIN.

53 B.C. DEATH OF CRASSUS - POMPEY & CAESAR COME TO BLOWS
58-51 B.C. CAESAR'S CONQUEST OF GAUL.

59 B.C. FIRST CONSULATE OF CAESAR

60 B.C. FIRST TRIUMVIRATE (POMPEY, CRASSUS, CAESAR)

66-61 B.C. CRASSUS AND CAESAR TRY TO SEIZE POWER IN POMPEY'S ABSENCE.

THE STORY OF
JULIUS CAESAR

During a time of **political** instability in Rome, the people celebrate Julius Caesar's victory over **Pompey**, their former leader. Officials representing ordinary Romans express **reservations** about the new leader. Caesar attends a festival and is **warned** to *Beware the ides of March*. He dismisses the **soothsayer's** warning as the rantings of a dreamer.

Cassius and Brutus are both **followers** of Caesar, but they think he is becoming too **powerful** and may abuse his position. Caesar is **suspicious** of Cassius, who begins to **persuade** Brutus that something must be done to **halt** Caesar's ambitions.

A frightened Casca walks the streets during a **storm** and tells stories of strange and unnatural **happenings,** which he believes to be a sign that the **gods** are upset. Cassius **ridicules** his fear and says that the strange happenings are warnings to beware of Caesar. He reveals that he has enlisted the support of several influential Romans in a **conspiracy**. Because Brutus is vital to the success of his treacherous plan, Cassius arranges for **letters** that appear to be from several writers to be **delivered** to Brutus urging him to act against Caesar.

Brutus struggles with his **conscience**, but decides that it is in the best interests of Rome if Caesar dies. The other **conspirators** visit Brutus to plan the assassination. Brutus's wife **Portia** is concerned about her troubled husband and asks him to confide in her.

The ides of **March** arrive and Caesar is due to go to the **Capitol** to be crowned. Storms, bad omens, and his wife Calphurnia's terrible **dreams** make him decide to stay home. Decius provides a flattering interpretation of Calphurnia's nightmares, however, and suggests that the senators might change their **minds** about crowning Caesar if he doesn't turn up. Ignoring these and further **warnings** from the soothsayer and Artemidorus, Caesar enters the Capitol, and the conspirators **stab** him.

Caesar's greatest **ally**, Mark Antony, is welcomed by Brutus, but

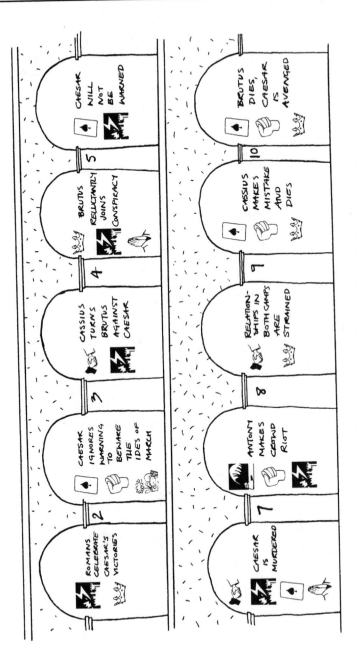

Cassius is wary of him. Antony pretends to join the assassins but privately intends to **avenge** Caesar's death. Brutus addresses the confused crowd and wins their **support** for the assassination, but Antony then cleverly turns them **against** the conspirators and incites them to riot.

Enjoying popular support in Rome, the **triumvirs** Antony, Lepidus, and Caesar's nephew, **Octavius,** plan to fight Brutus and Cassius. Brutus, still troubled by his conscience, sees Caesar's **ghost**. Two **battles** take place. Brutus and Cassius are **defeated** and save their **honor** by committing suicide. The triumvirs have seized **power** and avenged Caesar.

How much can you remember?

Try to fill in the words missing from this summary without looking back at the original. Feel free to use your own words if they have the same meaning.

During a time of _____ instability in Rome, the people celebrate Julius Caesar's victory over _____, their former leader. Officials representing ordinary Romans express _____ about the new leader. Caesar attends a festival and is _____ to *Beware the* _____ *of March*. He dismisses the _____'s warning as the rantings of a dreamer.

Cassius and Brutus are both _____ of Caesar, but they think he is becoming too _____ and may abuse his position. Caesar is _____ of Cassius, who begins to _____ Brutus that something must be done to _____ Caesar's ambitions.

A frightened Casca walks the streets during a _____ and tells stories of strange and unnatural _____, which he believes to be a sign that the _____ are upset. Cassius _____ his fear and says that the strange happenings are warnings to beware of Caesar. He reveals that he has enlisted the support of several influential Romans in a _____. Because Brutus is _____ to the success of his treacherous plan, Cassius arranges for _____ that appear to be from several writers to be _____ to Brutus urging him to act against Caesar.

Brutus struggles with his _____, but decides that it is in the best interests of Rome if Caesar dies. The other _____ visit

Brutus to plan the assassination. Brutus's wife _____ is concerned about her troubled husband and asks him to confide in her.

The ides of _____ arrive and Caesar is due to go to the _____ to be crowned. Storms, bad omens, and his wife Calphurnia's terrible _____ make him decide to stay home. Decius provides a flattering interpretation of Calphurnia's nightmares, however, and suggests that the senators might change their _____ about crowning Caesar if he doesn't turn up. Ignoring these and further _____ from the soothsayer and Artemidorus, Caesar enters the Capitol, and the conspirators _____ him.

Caesar's greatest _____, Mark Antony, is welcomed by Brutus, but Cassius is wary of him. Antony pretends to join the assassins but privately intends to _____ Caesar's death. Brutus addresses the confused crowd and wins their _____ for the assassination, but Antony then cleverly turns them _____ the conspirators and incites them to riot.

Enjoying popular support in Rome, the _____ Antony, Lepidus, and Caesar's nephew, _____, plan to fight Brutus and Cassius. Brutus, still troubled by his conscience, sees Caesar's _____. Two _____ take place. Brutus and Cassius are _____ and save their _____ by committing suicide. The triumvirs have seized _____ and avenged Caesar.

Picture this

? Here is the key point summary of *Julius Caesar* without the words. Can you add the missing points in words using the pictures to help you?

now that you know what's going on, take a break

PLOT SUMMARY

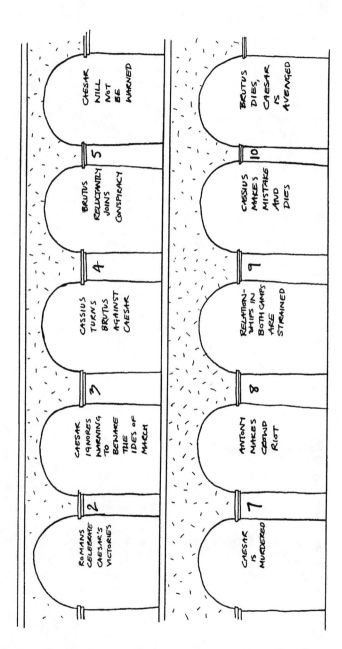

2 — ROMANS CELEBRATE CAESAR'S VICTORIES

3 — CAESAR IGNORES WARNING TO BEWARE THE IDES OF MARCH

4 — CASSIUS TURNS BRUTUS AGAINST CAESAR

5 — BRUTUS RELUCTANTLY JOINS CONSPIRACY

CAESAR WILL NOT BE WARNED

7 — CAESAR IS MURDERED

8 — ANTONY MAKES CROWD RIOT

9 — RELATIONSHIPS IN BOTH CAMPS ARE STRAINED

10 — CASSIUS MAKES MISTAKES AND DIES

BRUTUS DIES, CAESAR IS AVENGED

WHO'S WHO?

The Mini Mind Map above summarizes the character groups in *Julius Caesar*. Test yourself by looking at the full Mind Map on p. 23, and then copying the Mini Mind Map and trying to add to it from memory.

The characters in *Julius Caesar* bustle into the story and grab their share of the action. Unlike the way in which so many characters are presented in drama, few are introduced, described, and scrutinized for their personal qualities before they get involved in the action. Rather, the details of their lives and attitudes are drawn out of them as a result of the action. This makes Shakespeare's Romans very well-rounded, complex, and lifelike. They experience conflict within themselves and act with the inconsistency of real humans.
✪ How much do you think the fact that these people actually lived helps to make them so lifelike?

Julius Caesar

The legendary character after whom the play is named is murdered relatively early in the play. He appears in only three scenes, but he dominates the actions of others while he is alive, and continues to do so in death. Shakespeare presents him as both a demigod and an ordinary mortal.

11

THE FOREMOST MAN OF ALL THE WORLD

♠ Before his first appearance in Act 1, scene 2 we are told by the Tribunes that Caesar *may soar above the view of men*. Their disapproval of Caesar and the celebrating crowd prepares us for his entrance, and so Caesar's greatness is assumed from the start of the play. Anyone who speaks of him does so either with praise or envy at his achievements. The very mention of his name is enough to provoke comments that reinforce his stature. It is a common feature of dictators that they define the rules and limitations of the societies they govern, and so make strong and powerful leaders.

I AM CONSTANT AS THE NORTHERN STAR

Much of the praise for Caesar's greatness comes from him. He compares himself first to the North Star: *Of whose true-fixed and resting quality/ There is no fellow in the firmament* (Act 3, scene 1 (lines 67–68), and then to Mount Olympus, the mythical seat of the gods. Although he sounds boastful, his opinion of himself is echoed in the view that others have of him, and in the stature of the historical Caesar.

We are in no doubt that all stand in awe of Caesar. Antony says: *When Caesar says, "Do this," it is performed*. None of the characters fighting for power commands the same respect and unity, and before he is murdered, several of the conspirators are on bended knees before him, a courtesy and sign of respect that is not extended to any other character.

It is in keeping with Caesar the legend that he should refer to himself almost exclusively in the third person (by his name rather than "I" or "me"), even when he is alone with his wife. It is as if he gains strength and satisfaction from viewing himself as a great leader. His power lives on after his death through Antony and Octavius, however, as both Cassius and Brutus find to their cost.

That power and success may have begun to go to his head is demonstrated by his reason for staying away from the Capitol: *The cause is in my will: I will not come;/ That is enough to satisfy the Senate*. Just as quickly as Calphurnia has persuaded him, Decius works on him to go after all. Revealing ambition, the very quality that he is apparently killed for possessing,

Caesar simply cannot resist the idea that he may be crowned today. He is not an ungenerous man, however. He leaves money and parklands to the citizens of Rome that Antony is later anxious to recoup to fund his army.

I KNOW NO PERSONAL CAUSE TO SPURN AT HIM

Shakespeare also treats us to a view of Caesar that is not commonly reported in history books. He gives us an arrogant, fickle, and weak man prone to flattery and delusion. In almost the same breath he says to Antony: *...for always I am Caesar./ Come on my right hand, for this ear is deaf,* (Act 1, scene 2, lines 222–223). This statement first shows Caesar reinforcing his formidable public image and then Caesar the fallible man. He is seen is his nightgown, suffers from epilepsy, and is several times referred to as sickly and feeble. Shakespeare even makes him a poor swimmer, which was not in fact true of the historical Caesar.

HE IS SUPERSTITIOUS GROWN OF LATE

Caesar's first words reveal his belief in superstition. In the hope that his barren wife will become fertile, he tells her to stand in Antony's way as he runs at a fertility festival in the hope that she will become fertile. He immediately switches from his private belief in superstition to his rational public persona and dismisses as a dreamer the soothsayer who warns him to *beware the ides of March.*

This contradiction in Caesar's character comes up several times. At the start of Act 2, scene 2, Caesar is worrying about Calphurnia's nightmare in which he has been murdered, and instructs his priests to *present sacrifice,/ And bring me their opinions of success.* Calphurnia presents an entire collection of omens and oddities that echo his own concern, but as a ruler he chooses to disregard them.

He thinks that *things that threatened* will vanish at the sight of him, and that: *Danger knows full well/ That Caesar is more dangerous than he.* Despite this bravado Calphurnia soon persuades him to stay at home. In this scene he has tipped back and forth from superstitious ordinary mortal to invincible demigod.

Now try this

? Which of the following does Caesar compare himself to? Mount Olympus, hart, lion, snake, Northern Star, dog?

? How dignified was Caesar's death?

Brutus

Brutus is the honorable man with the noble mind. He becomes caught up in the momentum of Cassius's conniving against his good friend Caesar, and only makes up his mind to join the conspirators in the early hours of the day upon which Caesar is killed.

He is plunged into conflict within himself for ignoring his personal knowledge because it goes against his political ideals.

CAESAR'S ANGEL

We are often reminded that Brutus is well respected throughout Rome. He seems to be crucial to the success of the assassination, and Shakespeare presents him as the only character to have a conscience about the action he is about to take. For Brutus this is a moral issue. It may be true that Caesar was Brutus's father, which could be seen as explaining Caesar's great fondness for him. We do know that the real Brutus had supported Pompey rather than Caesar until his defeat. ✪ Why do you think Shakespeare left these details out of his play?

THE NOBLEST ROMAN OF THEM ALL

Brutus broods and agonizes over the decision he has to make about whether to join the conspirators. Perhaps he is flattered by the letters Cassius sends to cajole him into treachery because his arguments for betraying Caesar are weak. This would perhaps explain his tolerance of the devious Decius and the other blatantly ruthless conspirators. He decides that the only way to resolve the problem that Caesar **may** become is *by his death*. It is important that Brutus fears what Caesar might become rather than what he is – look at his speech in Act 2, scene 1, lines 20–36 in particular: *to speak truth of Caesar,/ I* *have not known when his affections swayed/ More than his reason.* It is this fear rather than fact and lack of clarity about what such an action might achieve that proves to be Brutus's downfall.

IF I DO LIVE,/ I WILL BE GOOD TO THEE

Brutus shows a soft and considerate side of his nature to Portia and to Lucius. He also speaks gently of Caesar to the conspirators on the eve of the assassination. It is not surprising, therefore, that Shakespeare makes Brutus recommend to the other assassins that they bathe in Caesar's blood. On both occasions, Brutus tries to elevate the murder to a ritual sacrifice rather than a mere political killing, out of a sense that it is a noble act.

This sense of ceremony also suggests that Brutus's soul is never quiet after he makes the decision to join the conspiracy.

BRUTUS, THOU SLEEP'ST: AWAKE, AND SEE THYSELF

Brutus's naïveté and lack of foresight is a blind spot. He is warned first by the conspirators that Antony should also be killed, but he underestimates Antony's power, popularity, ambition, and vengefulness. Cassius also warns Brutus not to trust Antony when, without consulting his fellow conspirators, Brutus allows Antony to speak at the funeral. Brutus does not anticipate the outcome, and acts too hastily, as he later does on the battlefield. He does not even mention privately how a new government might be structured. Although he is double-crossed by Antony at Caesar's funeral speech, he still deludes himself that *in all my life/ I found no man but he was true to me.*

BELIEVE ME FOR MINE HONOR

Unlike Antony, in his speech to the plebeians, Brutus is direct and appeals to the mob's understanding, even though his own reasoning is flawed and the plebeians have demonstrated that they do not reason soundly. He seems to think that swearing on his honor is enough to ensure the loyalty of the people. It proves not to be, particularly after Antony questions his honor.

Brutus is also domineering. He behaves arrogantly when he ignores Cassius's advice not to trust Antony, and again when he makes the decision to attack the armies of Antony and Octavius, which he does too soon. This leads to the mistake that Cassius makes and that leads to his death. His honor again suffers from a certain dual standard: He criticizes Cassius for bribery, but would be happy to use the money Cassius has raised in this way to fund his own army. He is angry that Cassius does not send him any of the money that he has raised, even though he disapproves of the means by which it was obtained.

I LOVE/ THE NAME OF HONOR MORE THAN I FEAR DEATH

Over Brutus's dead body Antony says: *All the conspirators save only he/ Did that they did in envy of great Caesar.* Despite good intentions for the future of Rome, Brutus has failed to realize that it is personal concerns that motivate most people, and that others will step in to occupy the vacuum left by Caesar.

By the time Brutus realizes that his death is inevitable, he has lost Caesar, Portia, Cassius, and Rome, but not his honor. He is even careful to find someone honorable to help him commit suicide.

Think about

?   How do you think Brutus feels as he draws his sword and Caesar says to him: *Et tu, Brute?*

?   Brutus says he will not be taken prisoner because he *bears too great a mind* (Act 5, scene 1, line 123). In view of how things turn out, how far do you agree with this statement?

?   Make a Mind Map of reasons for and against killing Caesar, as if you were Brutus.

take a short break before we meet Antony and the rest of the cast

Antony

Mark Antony, though a faithful follower and confidante of Caesar, is initially portrayed as a bit of a "party animal," a playboy *given/ To sports, to wildness, and much company*. He only begins to come into his own after Caesar's death when he becomes a key player.

A WISE AND VALIANT ROMAN

Antony soon proves to be a great opportunist. He does a great deal of quick thinking to arrive at a high-risk strategy for action after he has *Fled to his house amazed* after Caesar's death. He arrives at the Capitol to meet the assassins and see Caesar's body, after seeking an assurance of his personal safety, fully realizing that the assassins will think him a coward or a traitor for now siding with them. In order to win power, he has to persuade the assassins to trust him, and then gain access to the crowd and win their support. This is quite a gamble, calling for considerable nerve. Under pressure from Brutus the assassins accept Antony, unaware but not unsuspicious that he will soon double-cross them.

Antony is able to express his emotions with real heart in a way that Brutus's head never allows him to do. Antony gives vent to his grief and anger as soon as the conspirators depart. This show of passion and his predictions of the civil strife and bloodshed set the tone for the rest of the play.

A SHREWD CONTRIVER

Antony's speech to the plebeians over Caesar's body is masterful, calculating, and manipulative. He uses every shred of information he possibly can to win over the crowd, teases them with the will, and gets them to make the accusations that he himself only hints at. All this is said in tears topped with tragic pathos as he relives the murder and explains who made which wound, despite the fact that he wasn't there to witness it (see: The Exam Essay, p. 75).

He is delighted that he has set *Mischief* afoot and more of this ruthlessness quickly becomes apparent. He looks for ways to reduce the amount each citizen has been left by Caesar, readily agrees to kill off many other senators, including his own nephew, and speaks disparagingly of Lepidus, his ally.

Although he double-crosses Brutus, who calls him *a wise and valiant Roman,* he shows respect for him as he makes his final speech.

Cassius

Cassius passively dominates the first act. He is jealous of Caesar, has a cunning nature, and seeks self-advancement.

HE HAS A LEAN AND HUNGRY LOOK

We first meet Cassius at work on Brutus to become involved in the conspiracy. He judges well how best to sway Brutus, which includes using both fair means and foul, such as forging letters to flatter him. His objection to Caesar is based on envy, unlike that of Brutus, which is based on political belief. Caesar's suspicions and astute character analysis of Cassius confirm our own developing view of him very effectively (Act 1, scene 2, lines 208–222).

AWAY, SLIGHT MAN!

Cassius placates the frightened Casca in the storm, by giving the strange phenomena meanings that suit his motives, although even he eventually talks of seeing bad omens on the way to battle. He is a more artful and resourceful soldier than Brutus, able to raise funds in ways that to himself are justified by the means. Unlike his noble friend, he is no moral heavyweight. Through the weakness of his affection for Brutus, he is overruled by him several times against his own best judgment. He allows Brutus to let Antony outlive Caesar and deliver his damaging speech to the crowd, and decide tactics for the battle of Philippi.

CASSIUS IS AWEARY OF THE WORLD

Cassius' emotional instability and *rash humor* is most fully revealed in the quarrel scene (Act 4, scene 3) when he again offers to commit suicide rather than lose Brutus's affection. His fatal mistake is his *Mistrust of good success in battle.* He believes his side has been defeated and finally does kill himself.

Over to you

? What is particularly significant to Cassius about the day that he dies?

? What alternative did Antony have to pretending to make a deal with the conspirators?

? Look at this graph and see how Antony is introduced in Act 1, makes a brief appearance in Act 2, peaks in Act 3, and retains his position in the last two acts. Using colored pens, draw in the rise and fall of the other three main characters in the same way.

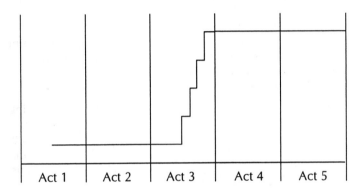

| Act 1 | Act 2 | Act 3 | Act 4 | Act 5 |

The women

Only two women, Portia and Calphurnia, appear in the play. Both are defined by their relationships to their husbands rather than in their own right. Their primary purpose is to give information about the private lives and attitudes of their men in contrast to their public images. The women are also caring influences, but they are incidental to the action rather than part of it. Both women show great concern for their husbands: Portia highlights the dilemma in which Brutus finds himself, and Calphurnia has visionary intuition that Caesar is in danger. In this respect they have more in common with the soothsayer and Artemidorus than any of the other characters.

RENDER ME WORTHY OF THIS NOBLE WIFE

There is a great deal of difference in the relationships the two women have with their husbands. The loyal Portia has to work hard to get Brutus to tell her what is on his mind. She asserts her right to know why he is troubled and Brutus, respecting her and her concern, does not let her stay on bended knees for long. Portia is worthy of sharing Brutus's confidences and, offstage, he tells her of the conspiracy. The emotional anguish that will send her to death soon begins. Her anticipation of doom, like Calphurnia's, is so great that she commits suicide long before it is necessary, because it is inevitable.

HOW FOOLISH DO YOUR FEARS SEEM NOW, CALPHURNIA!

Calphurnia's barrenness does not play any obvious part in the plot, but it may explain why she does not enjoy the same expression of affection as Portia does. Caesar, even when alone with her, refers to himself in the third person. He is not quick to let her get off her knees, and though he takes note of her concerns, he allows her to be overridden. The extreme accuracy of her prediction is chillingly intuitive. Unlike Portia, her fate is unknown in the play. History records that she lived on and supported Mark Antony, but this does not seem to interest Shakespeare.

What about the women?

? Which woman is more assertive, Portia or Calphurnia?
? Which husband shows the greater respect for his wife, Caesar or Brutus?
? When trying to keep the secret of the conspiracy, Portia says: *How hard it is for women to keep counsel* (Act 2, scene 4). Do you agree? How well do Portia and Calphurnia manage to keep secrets?

Lucius

Brutus's servant boy is like a son to him. Shakespeare makes him draw out a loving, fatherly side of Brutus for us to see. Lucius plays music, a symbol of harmony and order, but the respite it gives Brutus is brief (Act 4, scene 3). Lucius is also a symbol of Brutus's own lost youth and innocence.

The conspirators

The most important of these are Decius and Casca. Decius is so devious that he knows he can persuade Caesar to go out despite Calphurnia's warnings. He is scheming and quick-witted, which he demonstrates when he instantly thinks up a favorable interpretation of Calphurnia's dream. He has earlier diverted Caesar's attention from the letter Artemidorus wants to give to him. Decius smooths out the unexpected problems of the conspiracy.

Casca is a "fall guy," ready to use his brawn and be the first to stab Caesar. Most of the other conspirators and later officers in the armies of Brutus and Cassius are in the play to show extreme loyalty to their masters.

Octavius and Lepidus

After Caesar's death, these men played an important part in history. Lepidus is scorned by his ally Antony and we learn that his army is dispirited, an observation that Brutus seizes upon to try and gain an advantage over the triumvirs.

Caesar's nephew Octavius, although younger than Antony, is cool and assertive. He says that he crosses Antony, not to be awkward, but because he wants to do things his own way. He clears up the mess at the end without sentiment, and this sets the scene for the dominant role he will later play in history as Caesar Augustus. If Brutus's comment: *There is a tide in the affairs of men...* (Act 4, scene 3, lines 249–255) applies to any character in the play, it is Octavius whose real role in history was even greater than Caesar's.

The plebeians

These important street people play a crucial role in the development of the drama. Although in Caesar's Rome the republic was dominated by aristocrats, common people had achieved considerable rights to influence government. Tribunes really were elected to represent their interests to the Senate, and technically they had some power, although they were in practice manipulated by the senators, who came from wealthy families.

The plebeians had lived through much unrest before we meet them, and they show how much they need and lack stable leadership. They are ready to accept, more or less, anyone presented to them. They have been quick to transfer their praise from Pompey to Caesar when we meet them, and repeat this fickleness after Caesar's death when they first support Brutus and then switch allegiance to Antony.

Antony wins them over easily and uses them as instruments of his own game plan to attain power. They demonstrate that they are a dangerous force when they murder the poet Cinna just because he has the same name as one of the conspirators. The theme of disorder is largely developed by the plebeians.

Friends or foes?

? What do you think of Decius and Casca?
? If you had to choose one of the four main characters to spend an evening with, which one would you choose and why?
? Pick three characters from the play. Decide what star signs they might be and write horoscopes for them for March 15, 44 B.C.

now that you know who's who, take a break before going on to what's what

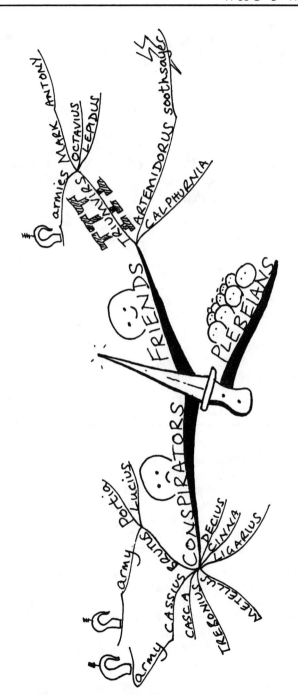

THEMES

A theme is an idea developed or explored throughout a work. The main themes of *Julius Caesar* are shown in the Mini Mind Map above. "Imagery" refers to the kind of word picture used to bring the themes to life. Test yourself on the themes by copying the Mini Mind Map, adding to it yourself, and then comparing your results with the full Mind Map on p. 35.

Friendship and betrayal

The betrayal of Julius Caesar by Brutus is one of the most famous in history. In Shakespeare's play, *Et tu, Brute?* is said in Latin by Caesar to his angel, Brutus. Caesar's surprise on discovering that Brutus is among the conspirators was reported by Plutarch: "Caesar did still defend himself against the rest, running every way with his body. But when he saw Brutus with his sword drawn in his hand, then he pulled his gown over his head and made no more resistance."

Although Caesar expresses his reservations about Cassius to his great friend Mark Antony (Act 1, scene 2, lines 208–222), he seems unaware of the threat from the other conspirators, all of whom claim to be his friends. Indeed these "friends" frequently call themselves brothers, and Brutus even refers to the dead Caesar as *my best lover* (Act 3, scene 2, line 47).

Dramatic irony occurs when we are aware of something that at least one character onstage knows nothing about. We are introduced to the reasons for murdering Caesar through the thoughts of Cassius and Brutus (Act 1, scene 2), and through Brutus's private thoughts as he sits up at night with a troubled mind (Act 2, scene 1).

That Caesar believes the conspirators to be his friends is made very clear when they arrive to collect him for the journey to the Capitol, apparently to be crowned (Act 2, scene 2). Shakespeare emphasizes how untrustworthy each of the main conspirators is by making Artemidorus prepare a note to warn Caesar about them (Act 2, scene 3).

The impending betrayal is emphasized by the unsettling influence of the storms and the supernatural.

After Caesar's death, Antony at first appears to turn traitor to his memory, but as soon as the conspirators leave, we hear his private thoughts and resolution to avenge the great man's fall. His words tell us what the remainder of the play will be concerned with. Antony then betrays the trust and friendship that Brutus has extended toward him when he turns the crowd against the conspirators at Caesar's funeral (Act 3, scene 2).

After Caesar's death, we are "flies on the wall" of the tents of the opposing armies. It is apparent that the alliance of the triumvirs is far from solid (Act 4, scene 1), and in the quarrel scene that follows (Act 4, scenes 2 and 3), the great friends Brutus and Cassius almost come to severe blows.

Although Antony never fails to respect Brutus (Act 5, scene 5, lines 74–81), Caesar's death prevents any friendship from developing between them. It is a final **irony** that Brutus, himself a traitor, says before he dies: *I found no man but he was true to me* (Act 5, scene 5, line 39). Brutus fails to recognize, or chooses to remain blind to, Antony double-crossing him. Perhaps this is because both he and Cassius, enjoying a loyalty they have not shown to Caesar, have difficulty persuading their fellow soldiers and friends to assist them in their suicides, the only honorable course of action for a Roman about to be taken prisoner.

Test yourself

? Which lines toward the end of Act 2, scene 2 suggest that Caesar believed the conspirators were his friends? How does scene 3 develop the idea of traitorous friends?

? Do you feel sorry for Caesar? What reasons can you think of for his deserving, or not deserving, to die the way he does?

Nobility and honor

The Roman Empire was largely founded upon an insistence on these qualities as personal and political ideals, and the characters in *Julius Caesar* show every evidence of it. As if to emphasize the fact that these men were shining examples of model Roman qualities, the names of Brutus, Caesar, and Antony are often prefixed with the word "noble." Look at Act 3, scene 2, or the battle scenes of Act 5 to see how often it appears.

The word "noble" is frequently applied to Brutus by all around him. We hear from Cassius that Caesar's love for Brutus is important to the success of the murder plot (Act 1, scene 2, lines 320–335) and the interchange between Cassius and Cinna soon afterward leaves us in no doubt that the high esteem in which Brutus is held throughout Rome ensures that his involvement is crucial (Act 1, scene 3, lines 144–146 and 166–169). It is ironic that the presence of these very qualities in Brutus contributes to the failure of the conspiracy by making him trust and underestimate Antony.

Brutus is very preoccupied with being noble and honorable. He tells us: *I love/ The name of honor more than I fear death* in the second scene. He refutes the need for the conspirators to take an oath on their pact to kill Caesar – to be Roman is enough; oaths are for *priests, cowards,* and *suffering souls* (Act 2, scene 1, lines 125–151). After Caesar's death he promises Antony safety upon his honor and his simple opening words to the crowd following Caesar's death include these: *Believe me for mine honor, and have respect to mine honor* (Act 3, scene 2, lines 15–16). Antony, with eloquence, turns this around in his emotional and stirring speech when he continually questions the honor of Brutus and the conspirators, and Caesar's ambition (Act 3, scene 2, lines 82–117).

When questioning Cassius's acceptance of bribes, Brutus claims to be *armed so strong in honesty* that he would not dream of taking bribes, although he would be happy to spend the money Cassius raises. This is something like a modern conservationist refusing to accept funds from a logging company unless someone first "launders" the funds. ✪ Do you think Brutus displays a double standard here?

Look at Brutus's exchange with Octavius just before battle:

> Octavius: *I was not born to die on Brutus' sword.*
> Brutus: *O, if thou wert the noblest of thy strain,*
> *Young man, thou couldst not die more honorable*
> (Act 5, scene 1, lines 62–64).

✪ Does it seem to you that Brutus is rather pleased with himself and his noble reputation (sharing some of Caesar's arrogance), or is he simply showing bravado and being condescending to a younger soldier in an attempt to undermine his confidence?

FALSE HONOR

The conspirators manage to convince themselves that killing Caesar is an *exploit worthy of the name of honor* (Act 2, scene 1, line 343). This is challenged, following Caesar's death, by the conspirators' confusion over what to do next and Antony's undermining of their reputations in his speech over Caesar's body. Then, in the play's final scene, Antony says of Brutus, *All the conspirators save only he/ Did that they did in envy of great Caesar* (Act 5, scene 5, lines 75–76).

Caesar is also frequently referred to as noble. In fact, Antony says over his corpse: *Thou art the ruins of the noblest man/ That ever lived in the tide of times* (Act 3, scene 1, lines 282–283). Ambition was considered a vice by the Elizabethans and here it is held up to be a negative quality possessed by, and responsible for, Caesar's death. As Brutus remarks: *as he was valiant, I honor him; but, as he was ambitious, I slew him* (Act 3, scene 2, lines 27–28).

Courage

Courage, and the *conquests, glories, triumphs, spoils* that could be expected to result from it, was also highly praised in Roman society. Shakespeare makes sure we see glimpses of courage in all the main characters and many of the minor ones.

Notice what Cassius says to the frightened Casca during the storm: *You are dull, Casca, and those sparks of life/ That should be in a Roman you do want, Or else you use not* (Act 1, scene 3, lines 60–62). We know that Caesar enjoyed many military successes and his valor shows in statements such as: *The valiant never taste of death but once* (Act, 2, scene 2, line 35). Comparing himself to Danger as if it is a person (**personification**), he says: *We are two lions littered in one day,/ And I the elder and more terrible* (Act 2, scene 2, lines 49–50).

The first thing Antony says as he arrives at the Capitol after Caesar's murder is that he is prepared to die then and there if the conspirators wish it. He is prepared to face up to death bravely rather than flee if it is inevitable. Generals in the armies of Brutus and Cassius who feature in Act 5 also show great courage, as do their two leaders, who face their inevitable deaths with great fortitude.

What do you think?

? What qualities do you consider to be the opposites of honor and nobility? Do any of the characters in *Julius Caesar* display these negative qualities?

? Which characters do you consider to be the most and least noble?

? How far do you agree with Caius Ligarius that killing Caesar was an *exploit worthy of the name of honor*?

? What tricks/literary devices does Antony use in his speech to the crowd, following Caesar's death, to undermine the conspirators' honor?

Fate and free will

How much of what happens to the characters is dictated by fate, and how much it is influenced by their own actions, is a strong theme throughout *Julius Caesar*. There are two main reasons why Shakespeare made so much of this. First, the play is about people who actually lived, and it is a fairly faithful account of what really happened to them. In this story with its basis in historical fact, Shakespeare reports the strange occurrences mentioned by Plutarch. In fact, he adds to them and uses them to create atmosphere and dramatic tension, and to **foreshadow** (warn us of) the trouble ahead. ✪ Can you think of other plays and modern films that use the same device?

Second, the Romans, like the Greeks before them, believed in many gods. Lacking scientific explanations for strange phenomena that are now better understood, they assumed the frightening events to be expressions of anger from gods displeased by human acts. Caesar's allusion to the North Star is also interesting because shortly after his death in 44 B.C. a comet appeared that was visible even by day. The Romans believed it to be Caesar's soul on its way to becoming a star.

THE CHAIN OF BEING

Although in Elizabethan England a belief in the existence of many gods had been replaced by belief in just one Christian God, people had not lost a sense of things being in the stars, or fated. It was also believed that all matter in the universe obeyed a certain order of hierarchy known as the "chain of being," with the gods and angels at the top, stones and metals at the bottom, and humans and animals somewhere in between. This order is reflected in Calphurnia's remark:

> *When beggars die, there are no comets seen;*
> *The heavens themselves blaze forth the death of princes.*
> (Act 2, scene 2, lines 31–33.)

Perhaps this is also a reference to the comet that blazed over Rome by day shortly after Caesar's death.

Against this background, it becomes clear that the storms and odd behavior of the animal kingdom, which so frighten Casca, and eventually even the rational Cassius, the augurer's omens, the soothsayer's warnings, and Calphurnia's nightmares, add authenticity to the story and capitalize on the audience's beliefs and superstitions. The audience already knows what will happen to Caesar and the strange and chilling phenomena contribute to the atmosphere and build up the suspense.

Shakespeare seems to be suggesting that some of the events recorded in the play are a result of fate. He complicates this explanation, however, by exploring moments when the individual could have made another choice, perhaps altering the course of history. Look at the way that Brutus arrives at the conclusion that Caesar must die purely by speculating on what Caesar may become. Moreover, Brutus's failure to foresee the crisis that Antony stirs up leads to his own downfall. ◗ How do you think history would have been changed if Brutus had remained loyal to Caesar?

CAESAR'S DILEMMA

Caesar, though *grown superstitious of late*, dismisses the soothsayer's warning as harmless dreaming and hovers between trusting Calphurnia's intuition and that of his augurers with his own desire for self-advancement. Shakespeare deliberately makes Caesar's dilemma hang in the balance for a few minutes as if to demonstrate again that the course of history might have been changed if Caesar had made a different decision. He appears to have free will, but is he fated to die that day? All it takes is Decius's manipulative skill to tip the balance. Caesar himself seems to believe that "what will be will be" when he says: *What can be avoided/ Whose end is purposed by the mighty gods?* (Act 2, scene 2, lines 27–28).

In the following short scene Artemidorus reads out the note he has prepared for Caesar and, echoing Caesar's words, closes the scene with:

> If thou read this, O Caesar, thou mayst live;
> If not, the Fates with traitors do connive.

Unlike the account in his source material, which describes the street as too crowded for Caesar to read Artemidorus's note, Shakespeare makes Caesar ignore it in an uncharacteristic display of concern for others rather than himself. ◗ Why do you think Shakespeare did this?

Order and disorder

Belief in a strict order of all things in the universe lingered on from the medieval period into Elizabethan times. Everything in the universe had its proper place, which perpetuated harmony between all things. If this harmony was upset, disorder would reign. Shakespeare makes much use of this theme of disorder, considerably embroidering Plutarch's account. Many of the strange phenomena described by Casca in Act 1, scene 3 stem from Plutarch, but the storms and Calphurnia's dreams seem to have been Shakespeare's invention.

The theme of disorder is introduced in the very first scene with Roman citizens giving themselves a day off work to celebrate Caesar's achievements. Rome is very much in a period of political transition and the people need a hero. Caesar is seen by the conspirators to threaten order by possibly becoming a tyrant. That this idea is as much an invention of the conspirators as a real threat soon becomes apparent. Conflict in the state is reflected in the discord of the heavens. Because the conspirators challenge the divine order of things, the heavens heave with disapproval in the form of storms, spontaneous fires, and animals behaving strangely.

BRUTUS'S PERSONAL DISORDER

A person was also considered to be a small reflection, or microcosm, of the larger heavens, or macrocosm. Notice the way Brutus compares his anguish in the period between deciding Caesar must be killed and actually doing it, to a nation plunged into civil war: *...and the state of man/ Like to a little kingdom, suffers then/ The nature of an insurrection* (Act 2, scene 1, lines 70–73). His personal knowledge of Caesar and political ideals are at odds, so Brutus experiences disorder in himself.

Disorder continues to threaten throughout Act 2 as Caesar ignores several warnings. It becomes apparent that the conspiracy is known by Portia, Artemidorus, and Popilius. This threatens to interrupt attempts to create a new order.

Act 3 could be called the act of disorder. Scene 1 witnesses Caesar's death, his assassins preparing, in Brutus's ironic words, to shout: *Peace, freedom and liberty!* (line 122) The assassins make no mention of what they have to offer the confused public instead. Caesar's death, far from bringing peace, freedom, and liberty, brings about the very disorder the conspirators claim to be ending. Ever a barometer of how things really are in Rome: *Men, wives, and children stare, cry out, and run,/ As it were doomsday (lines 107–108).* The scene closes with Antony's prophesy that: *Domestic fury and fierce civil strife/ Shall cumber all the parts of Italy (lines 289–290).*

A DISORDERLY CROWD

In Act 2, scene 3, we witness the crowd swing in allegiance from Caesar, to his assassins, and back to Caesar. They are so nervous and ready for action that all it takes is a strong orator to ignite their high spirits. By the end of the scene, Antony has them eating out of his hand, and ready to riot. Disorder reigns supreme as Act 3 closes with the plebeians in a final act of degeneration when they savage Cinna the poet just because his name is the same as one of the assassins.

In Act 4, the seeds of disorder are apparent in the inter-relationships among the cold-hearted triumvirs. Murdering senators and members of their own families as a matter of course indicates that they are losing the ability to reason and lack the remorse that Brutus feared was lacking in Caesar. Brutus fares little better in his relationship with Cassius, and his own spirit is plunged into further confusion when he sees or imagines Caesar's ghost. Only when Brutus and Cassius are defeated and Caesar's death is avenged does any sense of order return to Rome.

Ritual

Shakespeare uses ritual to create order in the play. He uses it not so much to reflect the rituals of political procedure or the highly organized style of Roman society, but as a tool his characters use to elevate their actions from morally dubious to worthy.

BRUTUS JUSTIFIES HIS ACTIONS

This is particularly true of Brutus, who in planning the assassination with his coconspirators says: *Let us be sacrificers, but not butchers... Let's carve him as a dish fit for the gods...*

We shall be called purgers, not murderers (Act 2, scene 1). Perhaps Brutus needs to persuade himself that his action will be justified. By placing an almost religious significance on the murder, he might also be conducting a good public relations exercise. Brutus's intention to treat Caesar with respect is echoed in his own memorial. Octavius says: *let us use him,/ With all respect and rites of burial* (Act 5, scene 5).

There are many references to blood in *Julius Caesar* but it comes as a surprise that Brutus should propose a bloodbath in Caesar's wounds (Act 3, scene 1). Since this image is Shakespeare's invention, it may attempt to show how Brutus justified his action to himself, and in the light of subsequent events, how far he was deluding himself.

Ill health

There is a great deal of illness in the first two acts of *Julius Caesar*. By the end of the second scene, we know that Caesar is a little deaf, *had a fever when he was in Spain*, shakes, groans, behaves *as a sick girl*, and swoons with *the falling sickness* (probably epilepsy). ✪ Why do you think Shakespeare made Caesar appear so sickly? Was it to suggest that he was not so great a threat to Rome as a younger, fitter man, or to demonstrate that he was an ordinary mortal?

AND SO IT CONTINUES...

Casca looks pale, Portia is told to protect her *weak condition* from the cold, Brutus claims to be sick, and Ligarius is introduced with the announcement: *Here is a sick man that would speak with you* (Act 2, scene 1, line 335). Both Calphurnia and Caesar, to begin with, see nothing wrong with taking a sick day on the ides of March.

Portia sends Lucius to check on Brutus who went *sickly forth*, and there are several references to being sick in spirit (as in Act 4, scene 3). Ill health seems to be replaced by death from Act 3 on, although we learn that Cassius's *sight was ever thick* in Act 5, scene 3. Many of the references to sickness carry a double meaning. They refer also to a sickness within the state, reflecting the Elizabethan belief in the person as microcosm and the universe as macrocosm. The individual body was seen as corresponding to the "body politic."

Test yourself

?   Which of the following are Caesar's true friends?
Brutus, Casca, Mark Antony, Trebonius, Artemidorus,
Cinna, Cassius.

?   Divide this circle into pieces of pie that reflect the
relative importance of each of the themes as you see
it. The theme you consider to be most important
should be the largest piece. Are there any other
themes in the play that you would like to add?

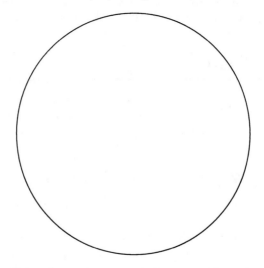

?   Using these pictures to help you, add words to
describe the themes they represent:

*now that you understand the play's themes,
take a break before reading about how
Shakespeare expresses them*

LANGUAGE, STYLE, AND STRUCTURE

The main features of *Julius Caesar* are shown in the Mini Mind Map above. Test yourself on them by copying the Mini Mind Map, adding to it yourself, and then comparing your results with the full Mind Map on p. 43.

Can you think of times when you use different types of language? For example, you probably use words with friends that you would not use with a teacher or parent. In the same way, Shakespeare varies the language he gives his characters according to who they are, who they are speaking to, and what they are speaking about.

The language used by Shakespeare in *Julius Caesar* is quite plain, whether or not the characters are speaking in prose or verse. It is the direct, straightforward language of people getting down to business. There is no need to use the rich images, metaphors, and allegory of lovers, for this is a play about war and power. The language is weighty rather than light, easy rather than complicated. *Julius Caesar* is written in a mixture of mostly verse and some prose.

Prose

Prose is flowing writing with no particular rules. It is conversational and less formal than verse. In Shakespeare, prose is usually used by such characters as lowly servants rather than educated gentlefolk. Caesar and the conspirators occupy important positions in society, and therefore they use **verse** most of the time, and certainly on formal occasions. They do use prose, however, when talking informally and confidentially.

The beginning of Act 1, scene 1 is written in the common prose of common people. When Brutus and Cassius talk confidentially with Casca in Act 1, scene 2 (lines 225–306), they talk in prose. When Brutus makes his speech to the plebeians (Act 3, scene 2), he tries to meet them on their own level by speaking in the prose they use themselves.

Verse

Shakespeare's formal language, called **blank verse**, is rather like poetry. It has a regular rhythm created mainly by the way words with different numbers of syllables are joined together and how words or sounds are repeated.

Blank verse has a tighter structure than prose. Most of the lines are regular, and they usually consist of five "iambic feet." A foot is a unit of syllables, one of which is stressed. An iambus is a foot of two syllables: *Friends, Ro/mans, coun/trymen,/ lend me your ears* (Act 3, scene 2, line 82). ❷ How many syllables are there in this line? Choose another speech in which the verse looks regular, and tap the beat. How many beats are there to each line? Now choose a speech written in prose. Does it have the same, consistent number of beats?

Imagery

Imagery is the use of words to create pictures, or images, in the viewer's or reader's mind. Imagery makes what is being said more effective, can make an idea more powerful, and can help create a mood. You will find examples of imagery on almost every page of Shakespeare. Images of blood, storms, metals, weapons, animals, and poisonous creatures are well used in *Julius Caesar.*

Images of weapons occur particularly often. These are appropriate in a play about a man's world of war and power struggles. Images of metals and stones also make several appearances. Shakespeare usually uses them to describe people who lack intelligence or desirable Roman qualities such as honor and nobility. As the crowd celebrates Caesar's victories in the opening scene, Marullus says: *You blocks, you stones, you worse than senseless things.* When Antony tries to win over the crowd from Brutus after Caesar's death, he says: *You are not wood, you are not stones, but men;* (Act 3, scene 2, line 154).

This imagery of materials links to Elizabethan beliefs about the strict order of the universe with the gods at the top of the hierarchy and stones and metals at the bottom. The attempt to turn ordinary metals into gold is called alchemy. Alchemy was practiced in medieval and Elizabethan times by a few dedicated individuals, usually more as a spiritual exercise than as a way to get rich. Shakespeare makes his characters compare the alchemist's mission with changing a person's base qualities into desirable ones.

Animal imagery is often used both by Caesar and others to describe him. Caesar compares himself to many creatures, most notably a lion (Act 2, scene 2, line 49). Brutus compares him to a snake (Act 2, scene 1, line 33), and after his death Antony compares him to a hunted deer (Act 3, scene 1, lines 229–230). Look at Cassius's two speeches in Act 1, scene 3 (lines 92–103 and lines 107–110). ❂ How many examples of imagery can you pick out?

Test yourself

? *He was quick mettle when he went to school.* Who is Brutus talking about, and what does he mean (Act 1, scene 2, line 308)?

? Who in the play uses prose and why?

? Decide which of the following is written in iambic feet (try tapping out the rhythm):

- *For who so firm that cannot be seduced?*
  (Act 1, scene 2, line 324)

- *Tis good. Go to the gate; somebody knocks.*
  (Act 2, scene 1, line 63)

- *Who is here so vile that will not love his country?*
  (Act 3, scene 2, line 34–35)

- *Are yet two Romans living such as these?*
  (Act 5, scene 3, line 110)

Irony

One kind of **irony** occurs when the opposite of what is meant is said, or when something turns out in the opposite way to what is intended. An example of irony in the turn of events is the error that Cassius makes on the battlefield when he mistakenly thinks that both his own and Brutus's army have been defeated, a simple but costly mistake made by someone whose ability to read situations accurately has seemed infallible before.

Irony is used in a slightly different way in Antony's speech to the crowd over Caesar's body (Act 3, scene 2). He repeatedly uses the word "honor" to suggest, on the face of it, that he really believes that Brutus and the other conspirators are *honorable men*. His use of the word is heavily laced with irony, however, because he actually believes that these men are traitors.

The final irony is that Caesar brought stability to Rome, not the disorder that Brutus fears so much. The opposite of what was intended by murdering Caesar is achieved.

Dramatic irony

This arises when the audience and perhaps some of the characters onstage know something that other characters do not. This helps to build suspense, and gives hints about what will happen next. A good example of **dramatic irony** is when the conspirators come to collect Caesar to go to the Capitol to be crowned (Act 2, scene 2, lines 113–137). Look at this scene, and then compare what you know to what Caesar knows. ✪ Who knows more about what is about to happen?

Personification

Shakespeare commonly describes something abstract as if it were a person. So, Fortune, when **personified,** becomes a woman who is also part of the order and harmony of the universe. Note Antony's remark when the rioting public have run Brutus and Cassius out of town: *Fortune is merry,/ And in this mood will give us anything* (Act 3, scene 2, lines 282–283). A few lines earlier he gives Mischief the same treatment.

Rhetoric

This is the term given to the art of effective or persuasive speaking or writing. The two speeches by Brutus and Antony immediately after Caesar's death are very good examples of how rhetoric is used to gain the support of the crowd for their own position (Act 3, scene 2). A question is said to be rhetorical when it is asked not for information but for effect. Both Brutus and Antony ask rhetorical questions in these powerful speeches. (See The Exam Essay, p. 75.)

History or tragedy?

Although the play was originally called *The Tragedie of Julius Caesar*, it does not share all the usual characteristics of Shakespeare's later and more famous tragedies: *Macbeth*, *King Lear*, *Hamlet,* and *Othello*. It borrows from the style but mixes it with the style of Shakespeare's earlier historical plays. We know that Caesar actually was killed on the ides of March. We witness the way he goes to his death, an event about which we already know, rather than wondering if he will die, which is quite different and more typical of tragedy. Shakespearean tragedy usually has the following characteristics:

It focuses on one important, noble person with a flawed character

In *Julius Caesar* the tragic elements apply not only to Caesar but also to Brutus and Cassius. Caesar is flawed by his arrogance, which might otherwise have saved him, and Brutus is flawed by his naïveté and underestimation of human nature and personal greed. Cassius tends to be hotheaded and jumps to conclusions. ✪ Why do you think the tragic heroes are usually men?

The tragedy is usually brought on by a character's own actions

Caesar is not directly responsible for his own death; he is the subject of a conspiracy that is as much about other people's self-advancement as it is about either his own motives or shortcomings. In tragedies of one person's downfall, the audience tends to become emotionally involved in the anguish that that character experiences. In *Julius Caesar* we are more aware that we are watching an interpretation of the lives of characters, the outcome of which we already know.

The tragic hero dies after great suffering

Not so if the hero is Julius Caesar. On the contrary, he has been enjoying praise following his great military success. The drawing of Brutus's character borrows more from this feature of tragedy. He experiences a troubled conscience in deciding what to do about the problem of Caesar, and cannot go back once Antony has turned the public against him. He loses everything.

Our sympathies are aroused

We never have a sense of great pity for any of the characters in *Julius Caesar*, such as is aroused by Shakespeare's great tragedies.

It conveys a sense of forces greater than mortals

Although *Julius Caesar* is about the actions of men, Caesar's status is godlike. Storms, omens, and fate suggest divine intervention. Against these forces, mortals are powerless.

It often involves a chance event or twist of fate that leads to downfall

In this play, the main example is Cassius's mistake on the battlefield. Chance happenings are not really a feature of *Julius Caesar*. Most things are very calculated.

It involves conflict.

The play shares this characteristic with the other tragedies.

Structure

In literature, **structure** refers to the framework for piecing the parts of the work together. *Julius Caesar* is a dramatized interpretation of a true story, an account of domestic drama, political assassination, and power struggles. Act 1 sets the scene and introduces most of the plot, themes, and characters. Act 2 develops the plot and the themes and reveals more about the characters and the relationships between them. We are becoming involved and want to know what will happen next.

By Act 3, the character the play is named after is killed. Far from being an anticlimax, however, a new story begins, that of the struggle for power between Antony and Brutus. The heroism and conflict in the battle scenes maintains suspense until the final resolution of the power struggle and the conclusion of all matters introduced earlier in the play.

PACE AND SUSPENSE

Pace is increased by a fast-moving plot, and suspense is developed in several ways. Portia's nerves put us on edge in Act 2, scene 4, and the warnings from both the soothsayer and Artemidorus keep up the momentum in the following scene. Because the soothsayer has told Portia that people on the streets *Will crowd a feeble man almost to death* (Act 2, scene 4, line 42), we expect the attack on Caesar to take place before he reaches the Capitol. Instead, we are presented with the possibility that the conspiracy will fail because Atemidorus and now Popilius have heard about it.

Setting and atmosphere

The first two acts of *Julius Caesar* are set in Rome, the political seat and heart of the Empire and setting for all plotting and scheming. Brutus's orchard is an appropriate setting for the private thinking he needs to do, and to hold a secret meeting to discuss the assassination (Act 2, scene 1). The final two acts follow the armies of the triumvirs and Brutus and Cassius to their battlesites.

In Act 3, there is a sense that anything might happen because a big event has touched the plebeians' lives and they are in the mood to riot.

Storms and strange phenomena in nature help to create the atmosphere, emphasize the developing conspiracy against Caesar in Act 1, scene 3, and act as a backdrop to Caesar's impending death in Act 2, scene 2. Just as earthly matters are troubled and treacherous, so the heavens will not be still and calm.

now take a break before beginning the Commentary

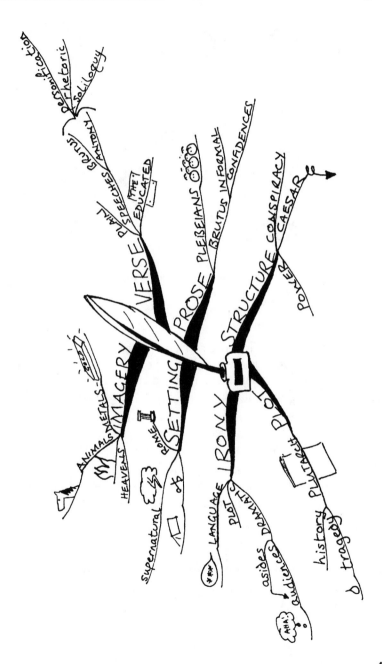

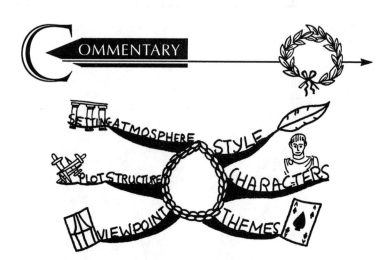

The Commentary looks at each scene in turn, beginning with a brief preview that will prepare you for the scene and help in last-minute review. The Commentary discusses whatever is important in the section, focusing on the areas shown in the Mini Mind Map above.

Wherever there is a focus on a particular theme, the icon for that theme appears in the margin (see p. x for key). Notice also the Style and Language sections. Being able to comment on style and language will help you to get an "A" on your exam.

You will learn more from the Commentary if you use it along with the play itself. Read a scene from the play, then the corresponding Commentary section, or the other way around.

Remember that when a question appears in the Commentary with a star ✪ in front of it, you should stop and think about it for a moment. And remember to take a break after completing each exercise.

Act 1 *scene* 1

- ◆ Flavius and Murellus question ordinary Romans.
- ◆ Murellas scolds the cobbler (shoemaker) and the carpenter.

FLAVIUS AND MURELLUS QUESTION ORDINARY ROMANS (LINES 1–35)

The play opens on a street in Rome where a crowd has gathered. The first character to speak is Flavius. He and Murellas are Tribunes, magistrates responsible for representing the interests of ordinary Romans. They are the only named characters in the scene. By not naming the others, Shakespeare makes them represent all common Romans.

Flavius asks the carpenter why he is taking a holiday on a working day and reminds him that it is not fitting for a manual worker to be wearing his best clothes on such a day. Rather, he should indicate the job he does by wearing work clothes or carrying tools.

The cobbler avoids giving a direct reply, and is sarcastic instead. He makes a **pun** (a play on words that sound the same but have different meanings, both of which are somehow appropriate). Here the wordplay is on "soul" and "sole." He says that he mends *bad souls*. Although literally he means that he mends shoes, he implies that by rejoicing instead of working, he is repairing people's tired spirits. ❂ What words do the Tribunes use to show that they think the cobbler is sarcastic (lines 16–21)?

Eventually, the cobbler reveals the reason for the rejoicing, but not before he makes another joke about creating work for himself by leading these *men about the streets* so that they will wear out their shoes. He says the crowd is celebrating Caesar's latest triumphs.

MURELLAS SCOLDS THE COBBLER AND THE CARPENTER (LINES 36–60)

Murellas makes a speech scolding the men for being so quick to shift their loyalty from Pompey (the previous Roman leader) and his sons to the newly conquering Caesar (lines 32–60).

He asks if capturing prisoners and reveling in the glory is really worth celebrating, and accuses the men of being without sensitivity and compassion by comparing them to blocks and stones. Only recently they have similarly rejoiced in the victories of Pompey, and now they rejoice in the victory of the man who slew his fellow Roman rather than foreign enemies. Murellas dismisses them for showing this ingratitude. **45**

❍ What do you think this speech says about the ability of the common people to understand affairs of state?

Flavius and Murellas agree to go in different directions to the government building known as *the Capitol*, to take down the many icons and symbols of Caesar that they come across on the way, despite extra decorations due to simultaneous festivities associated with the Feast of Lupercal, an annual fertility festival. The two are worried that if Caesar becomes too important, he will become a ruthless ruler.

The scene establishes the idea that the common citizens of Rome have a poor understanding of their long-term interests and are fickle in their allegiance to their leaders. The Tribunes, who have a better understanding of Roman politics, are suspicious of their new leader. From the start we are aware of dangerous unrest in Rome, a theme that is developed throughout the play.

STYLE AND LANGUAGE

The type of language Shakespeare uses in this first scene continues throughout the play. It is direct and simple rather than romantic, lyrical, or descriptive. This is appropriate language with which to equip a society that prided itself on logical, straightforward reasoning and practical advances in many areas of life. Shakespeare makes us aware of the pride and self-assurance possessed by common Romans by making the interaction between them and the Tribunes quite balanced; the artisans do not humble themselves to the representatives of their interests.

Note that in some published versions of the play, the cobbler chooses the word *holy-day*, from which the word that Flavius uses, *holiday*, is derived. This has the effect of introducing Caesar as a kind of god as well as a man (lines 2 and 34). **❍** What does Flavius say at the end of the scene that reinforces this view of Caesar?

That the gods are important and taken very seriously is demonstrated when Murellas suggests that they should: *Pray to the gods to intermit the plague/ That needs must light on this ingratitude* (lines 59–60).

Shakespeare reveals a great deal about the attitude of the commoners by referring to *their basest mettle* (line 66), as well as comparing them to the common, inanimate raw materials used in construction. They are the basic building blocks of Roman society, and base metal was the cheap and common material that alchemists hoped to transform into gold. A pun on the word *guiltiness* (line 67) reinforces the idea – "gilt" is a poor imitation of real gold.

The cobbler uses another play on words earlier: *all* and the tool, *awl*, and in the next line *withal* (lines 24–26).

Act 1 *scene* 2

◆ Caesar is warned to beware the ides of March.
◆ Cassius compliments Brutus.
◆ Cassius examines Caesar's character.
◆ Caesar tells Antony he suspects Cassius.
◆ Casca reports Caesar's refusal to accept the crown.

♠ This long scene plants the idea that fate will seal Caesar's future, and hints at the method of his undoing through an airing of the doubt and unrest in the minds of Caesar's compatriots. Because the play is based on historical fact, few people in the audience would be unaware of what happened to Caesar. The interest therefore, is in how Shakespeare interprets Caesar's downfall. Most of the main characters are introduced in this scene.

CAESAR IS WARNED TO BEWARE THE IDES OF MARCH (LINES 1–29)

♠ Mark Antony is about to run the Holy Chase as part of the Feast of Lupercal. We learn that Caesar's wife, Calphurnia, has produced no children, and that if Antony touches her during his run, she may be blessed with fertility.

A soothsayer, in a voice that chills Caesar with its shrillness, tells him to *Beware the ides of March*. The "ides" is the name given to the fifteenth day of some months, the day on which accounts would be settled. ❍ In what way is this an appropriate day for Caesar's death? We are soon to learn that Caesar may be deaf in one ear, and to make sure that the audience does not miss the significance of the prediction from what Caesar dismisses as a dreamer, it is said three times.

CASSIUS COMPLIMENTS BRUTUS (LINES 30–96)

Cassius tells Brutus that he has been avoiding eye contact and behaving coldly toward him. Brutus explains that his conscience is troubled, he does not feel himself, and that his manner is nothing personal. Cassius tries to boost Brutus by telling him how worthy he is and how well he is respected.

Brutus seems to sense that Cassius has a hidden agenda, as Cassius continues to assert his regard. A flourish – probably of trumpets or pipes – sounds and the crowd cheers. Brutus lets down some of his guard and gives away the information that he has fears about Caesar becoming an absolute ruler, despite the love he has for him. The elation of the crowd and the fears of the elite are evidence of the tension that will lead to civil unrest in Rome.

The contradiction that is bothering Brutus thus explained, he wants to know what Cassius wants of him, or wants to tell him, adding that he would rather die than sacrifice his honor.

CASSIUS EXAMINES CAESAR'S CHARACTER (LINES 97–187)

In a lengthy speech, Cassius observes that Caesar is no different from them, and tells Brutus of the time when he rescued Caesar from drowning in the River Tiber after Caesar had suggested the plunge for a dare. He remarks on the extreme inappropriateness of a man as weak as Caesar becoming so important in contrast to himself when he says: *And this man/ Is now become a god, and Cassius is / A wretched creature* (lines 122–124). ✪ What other example does Cassius present to Brutus as evidence of Caesar's unsuitability as a leader?

Cassius continues to present arguments to Brutus that treat Caesar as a man no more ordinary or extraordinary than they. Brutus acknowledges Cassius's arguments, says he will think about them, since they are matters on his mind already, but adds that he does not wish to discuss it further. Cassius is pleased to have made the progress he has in stirring Brutus to rise against Caesar.

CAESAR TELLS ANTONY HE SUSPECTS CASSIUS (LINES 188–224)

Brutus observes that Caesar and his followers seem troubled. He and Cassius resolve to ask Casca what has happened at the Capitol.

Caesar confides to Antony that he is suspicious of Cassius. What he says is a shrewd and intuitive assessment of the concealed truth. Caesar recognizes Cassius's *lean and hungry look*, and guesses correctly what the audience already knows: *Such men as he be never at heart's ease/ Whiles they behold a greater than themselves/ And therefore are they very dangerous.*

CASCA REPORTS CAESAR'S REFUSAL TO ACCEPT THE CROWN (LINES 225–334)

Casca tells Brutus and Cassius that at the Capitol Caesar was three times offered the crown by Antony, and three times refused to take it, although, in Casca's opinion, he was very tempted.

Caesar then had an epileptic seizure, and, upon recovering, offered the people *his throat to cut*. The display is a showy performance designed to draw loyalty from a fickle public. The epileptic seizure, construed here as a sign of weakness, is the reason for Caesar and his followers appearing troubled when they leave the Capitol, although public acceptance of the new leader seems guaranteed.

Casca goes on to demonstrate how Caesar's importance is growing when he says that for removing the decorations from Caesar's images about Rome, Flavius and Murellas are *put to silence.* ❍ What do you think this means?

The scene closes with arrangements being made to meet again. When Casca and Brutus leave the stage, Cassius reveals to the audience his hope that the noble Brutus may be turned against Caesar who trusts him. The image of metal is again used to describe this possibility. Cassius resolves to deliver to Brutus, anonymously, letters that appear to come from different writers praising Brutus. He hopes to win Brutus's support in unseating Caesar *or worse days endure.*

Act 1 scene 3

◆ Casca speaks of strange happenings.
◆ Cassius advances the conspiracy against Caesar.

CASCA SPEAKS OF STRANGE HAPPENINGS (LINES 1–41)

The scene is set in the evening during a thunderstorm, a dramatic device to indicate that trouble is brewing. It provides a fitting backdrop to Casca's speech about the strange happenings he has witnessed.

He tells Cicero that he has seen odd things before, but what he has just seen is so unusual that the gods must be upset, and that these things are bad omens.

CASSIUS ADVANCES THE CONSPIRACY AGAINST CAESAR (LINES 42–169)

The clever and scheming Cassius goes about persuading the frightened Casca to join the conspiracy against Caesar. He says that true Romans are not afraid of such phenomena and compares them to the way Caesar is exercising his increasing power.

From Casca we learn that the Senate might crown Caesar king on the following day. Cassius continues to criticize Caesar and argues eloquently for rising against him. On receiving an assurance of Casca's support, Cassius reveals that other important Romans are part of the plot.

Cinna joins the two conspirators, talks also of the strange happenings, and agrees to deliver a letter to Brutus. Cassius reveals that a growing number of conspirators are planning to meet. The scene closes with Cassius and Casca reflecting on how important it is to persuade Brutus to join them, and that securing his support is increasingly likely.

 ### STYLE AND LANGUAGE

Some of the language richest in imagery occurs in this scene full of visions of the unnatural behavior of animals and the elements.

The reference to alchemy appears again when Casca talks of transforming Brutus into a conspirator at the end of the scene.

Test yourself

? What behavior does Flavius recommend to the working people as more fitting than rejoicing for Caesar?

? Do you think Cassius is jealous of Caesar? Give reasons for your answer.

? In your own words, describe the strange behavior of living things that Casca thinks are omens.

take a break before you join the conspiracy

Act 2 *scene* 1

◆ Brutus justifies his decision.
◆ The conspirators advance the plan.
◆ Portia confronts the troubled Brutus.

BRUTUS JUSTIFIES HIS DECISION (LINES 1–72)

A sleepless Brutus sits alone in his orchard and instructs his servant, Lucius, to light a candle. We seem to join him in midthought as he opens with: *It must be by his death: and for my part/ I know no personal cause to spurn at him/ But for the general* – Caesar must die in the interests of the greater good rather than for any personal reason. Brutus explains to the audience, while justifying his resolve to himself, that a person in Caesar's position is dangerous if he rules without compassion. Brutus adds that on achieving power, a corrupt person does not look back on the humble beginnings that first gave rise to gaining power. Brutus has no real reason to support the conspiracy but seems to be searching hard for one.

Lucius gives Brutus the letter that Cinna has secretly delivered, and is asked to check if the coming day is March 1. This is confusing, because we know that the ides of

March is on March 15, and we would expect Brutus to know, too. He shows no surprise when Lucius announces that *March is wasted fifteen days.* Perhaps Shakespeare or someone copying the play made a mistake, or perhaps Brutus is confused. ❂ What do you think?

There is enough light from the storm for Brutus to read the letter. Ironically, since Brutus is suffering from insomnia, it begins: *Brutus, thou sleep'st: awake and see thy self* (line 48). The letter writer's wish has been granted; Brutus has made up his mind to join in the conspiracy against Caesar. This decision has not been arrived at easily, however. Brutus is a reluctant conspirator who feels he is stuck in a bad dream.

THE CONSPIRATORS ADVANCE THE PLAN (LINES 73–252)

The conspirators, dressed to conceal their identities, arrive at Brutus's house. They are welcomed, and the assassination is discussed. Throughout this meeting Brutus urges restraint from barbarity. First he rejects Cassius's suggestion that they should swear an oath on their decision to act, saying that the word of a Roman is oath enough. Then he resists the suggestion of involving Cicero, a respected old man whose endorsement of the plan would balance any criticism the others may encounter for being younger men, and finally by turning down the suggestion that Mark Antony should also be killed.

Just as swearing an oath was Cassius's idea, so the argument for killing Mark Antony is developed, though not suggested by him. Ironically, his fear that Antony's: *means/ If he improve them, may well stretch so far/ As to annoy us all* (lines 171–173) is prophetic of the way events actually do unfold.

Brutus underestimates Antony when he dismisses him as *but a limb of Caesar,* but argues well that one death is enough. He attempts not only to show due respect to Caesar, but to condone the impending act as almost a religious sacrifice. ❂ What words does Brutus use to explain how the conspirators should be seen and that contrast with *butchers* and *murderers?*

In preparation for the next scene, Shakespeare makes the conspirators discuss the likelihood of seeing the superstitious Caesar at the Capitol later in the day. Decius displays his deviousness when he outlines how he can manipulate Caesar to do as he wishes. The group decide to enlist the support of Caius Ligarius who has upset Caesar by speaking well of Pompey. Brutus urges them to try to act normally with Caesar.

PORTIA CONFRONTS THE TROUBLED BRUTUS (LINES 253–363)

 For the first time in the play, a woman speaks. Portia knows her husband is troubled, and will not accept his explanation of physical sickness. She has seen the fellow conspirators and demands to know what is really troubling him, explaining that she has a right to know, which comes to her as part of their marriage vows. Brutus respects her and treats her as an equal; he will not let her kneel while imploring him to confide in her. He agrees to tell her what is going on soon, and asks the gods to make him worthy of her.

The scene closes with a visit from Caius Ligarius, the sick old man who agrees to join the conspirators. Thunder can still be heard on this troubled night.

STYLE AND LANGUAGE

Imagery of poisonous snakes is used in this scene by Brutus to describe Caesar. The image will be picked up again several times later on.

Think of the way that Death the reaper is often pictured. ❂ Is there anything about the way the conspirators are dressed that reminds you of it (lines 79–80)?

Act 2 scene 2

◆ Calphurnia persuades Caesar to stay at home.
◆ Decius makes Caesar change his mind.

CALPHURNIA PERSUADES CAESAR TO STAY AT HOME (LINES 1–60)

As in the previous scene, when Portia shows care and concern for her husband, this scene also eavesdrops on the private relationship between Caesar and his wife, Calphurnia. She also demonstrates care and concern for her husband.

The storm continues, and Calphurnia has had nightmares about Caesar being murdered. She reminds her husband of the strange behavior of the natural world that Casca detailed in Act 1, scene 3, and Caesar in his self-important way reasons *that death.../ will come when it will come.*

As Caesar keeps Calphurnia on bended knees, she again appeals to him to stay at home. On hearing that an animal, specially sacrificed for the purpose of finding omens, has no heart, Caesar agrees to do so.

DECIUS MAKES CAESAR CHANGE HIS MIND (LINES 61–137)

Caesar arrogantly thinks that his wish to remain at home is sufficient explanation for the Senate of his absence. He is quick to change his mind, however, when the devious Decius gets to work on him as he has said he will in the previous scene. He points out that the senators may change their minds if they do not crown Caesar today, and he also offers Caesar another explanation for Calphurnia's prophetic dream, which undermines and mocks her sound intuition.

The scene ends with the arrival of the conspirators and the loyal Mark Antony who have come to collect Caesar to take him to the Capitol – and his death.

Word workout

?   What does Brutus say that suggests he is not proud of the conspiracy?

?   What words does Decius use to mock Calphurnia's prophetic dream?

?   Describe Decius's interpretation of Calphurnia's dream in your own words.

Act 2 *scene* 3

◆ Artemidorus reads his note to Caesar.

Artemidorus enters for the first of two brief appearances in this short scene. He speaks only to the audience, listing each of the conspirators and giving a reason why Caesar should be suspicious of each one. His purpose is to further advance the plot, and add to the excitement. We wonder what will happen if he manages to pass on the note and reveal the conspiracy.

Act 2 *scene* 4

◆ Portia is distressed by concern for Brutus.

Portia is so worried about Brutus that she almost sends Lucius to find him without any reason. This shows us how distressed she is. Her failure to instruct Lucius also reflects her lack of information about what is going on.

The arrival of a soothsayer contributes to the sense of imminent danger to Caesar, particularly when he describes the narrow streets that would *crowd a feeble man almost to death* as Caesar travels to the Capitol.

Portia, trying to keep her concerns secret from Lucius, finally sends him to Brutus with no real mission, but to try to gather information.

Test yourself

?   Look up the reason given by Artemidorus for why Caesar should beware of Caius Ligarius (scene 3).

?   In Act 2, scene 4, Portia speaks of a woman's qualities several times. Describe them in your own words.

treat yourself to a break before the bloodbath

Act 3 *scene* 1

◆ The conspirators prepare to kill Caesar.
◆ Caesar is murdered.
◆ Antony meets the assassins and mourns Caesar.

THE CONSPIRATORS PREPARE TO KILL CAESAR (LINES 1–83)

As Caesar and the conspirators arrive at the Capitol, the audience is reminded by the soothsayer that *The ides of*

March are come/ ...but not gone. Artemidorus, the other voice of warning, is diverted from his mission to give Caesar the letter he read out to the audience in Act 2, scene 3, and so Caesar's fate is sealed.

Brutus and Cassius are temporarily flustered when Popilius encourages their enterprise. He is not one of the conspirators, but seems to know of their intentions anyway. The pair watch Popilius in conversation with Caesar and decide that their mission is still secret. The preparations for the assassination are completed when Trebonius *draws Mark Antony out of the way.*

Shakespeare makes Cinna tell us that Casca will strike the first blow to Caesar. Metellus appeals to Caesar to allow his banished brother to return to Rome, but Caesar will not be moved. Brutus and Cassius also appeal to Caesar, but in what is his last speech, he will not relent.

It is significant that in their appeals to a man they are about to kill, these three men kneel. It emphasizes Caesar's power and greatness as a ruler – they cannot be on equal terms while he is alive. Caesar reinforces this by saying he is above ordinary men and has no equal in the universe, except perhaps the North Star, an eternal fixed point and guide to all. Also note that Caesar's stubborn position probably helps to strengthen the conspirators' resolve and gives them a reason to crowd around him.

CAESAR IS MURDERED (LINES *84–162*)

Caesar is stabbed, and the assassins talk about proclaiming liberty in the streets.

As they hear how frightened Antony and other Romans are on learning of Caesar's death, Shakespeare makes Brutus bear out Calphurnia's dream by suggesting that they should face the public bathed in Caesar's blood.

As they prepare to leave the Capitol, Antony's servant arrives. He says that Antony honors Brutus and is prepared to follow him, but wants to know why Caesar has been killed. He also seeks a guarantee that he will not be harmed, as seems likely since he was Caesar's ally. The assurance given, the servant leaves. Brutus and Cassius briefly exchange their opposite opinions of Antony. ❷ Who thinks what (lines 159 – 162)?

ANTONY MEETS THE ASSASSINS AND MOURNS CAESAR (LINES *163–324*)

Brutus welcomes Antony, who says he does not understand why the assassins have killed Caesar. Because he was Caesar's ally, he offers himself up to be killed. Brutus assures him that they intend him no harm and Cassius promises him a role in the shaping of the new regime. Brutus asks Antony to wait until they have calmed the frightened public for a full explanation.

Antony goes on to shake the bloody hands of each assassin, and says that in joining them they must think of him as either a coward or a flatterer. He becomes distracted from the assassins as he apologizes to Caesar's spirit for now betraying him, and mourns him. ❷ What image does Antony conjure up to describe Caesar's fate (lines 225 – 230)?

Antony repeats that he will join the assassins if they can justify their action against Caesar. Brutus assures him that they have such good reason that even if Antony were Caesar's son, he would agree.

Antony asks if he can present the body to the people and speak at the funeral, a request that Brutus is happy to grant but that makes Cassius suspicious. In an aside between these two, Brutus reasons that allowing Antony to speak will make the assassins seem all the more reasonable and justified. Antony agrees to the conditions set out by Brutus for the content of his speech, and is left alone with Caesar's body.

 Antony is far more emotional in the **soliloquy** (a speech spoken by an actor alone onstage as if thinking aloud) that follows than he was when with the assassins. He prophesies that Italy will descend into turmoil and bloodshed now that Caesar is dead, and he swears revenge.

The scene closes with a servant delivering the news that Caesar's ally Octavius is on his way to Rome at Caesar's request before he died. Antony prepares to send the servant back after his funeral speech with instructions for Octavius to wait until it is safe.

STYLE AND LANGUAGE

After two acts in which concerns about Caesar have been presented, and the conspiracy planned, Act 3 sees Caesar's assassination, and establishes the nature of the trouble that follows. It is unusual to kill off a character after whom a play is named so soon, and Shakespeare has to find a way to keep up the dramatic tension. He does this by making Antony emerge as a more forceful character than he has previously seemed to be and shifts from the problems raised by a person to the problems facing the state. The assassination has achieved little because Antony and Octavius move into the political position that Caesar held.

If, why, and what

? If you were directing the play, would you make Caesar's remark, *Et tu, Brute?* ("And you, Brutus?"), a statement of surprise that Brutus has stabbed him or an invitation to Brutus to join in? Why?

? Why did all the conspirators stab Caesar rather than just one of them?

? Why does Antony shake hands with the assassins?

? What three conditions does Brutus make to Antony about his speech at Caesar's funeral (lines 269 – 276)?

Act 3 *scene* 2

◆ Brutus wins the support of the crowd.
◆ Antony turns the crowd against Brutus.

BRUTUS WINS THE SUPPORT OF THE CROWD (LINES 1–81)

Brutus, emerging as a new leader, sends some of the crowd off with Cassius to hear the reasons for killing Caesar. Four common people, or plebeians, as Shakespeare calls them, representing many more, gather to hear Brutus speak. He simply says that his great love and respect for Caesar is as deep as any man's, but that Caesar was ambitious and would have made the Romans slaves rather than free men. In an echo of the opening scene, in which the fickle public is shown to switch allegiance from Pompey to Caesar effortlessly, the people are quick to be influenced against their new hero by Brutus. He asks them to wait and listen to Antony, who enters carrying Caesar's body.

ANTONY TURNS THE CROWD AGAINST BRUTUS (LINES 82–287)

A passionate Antony then dominates the stage for the rest of the scene. He handles the crowd cleverly, like a performer, holding back information until exactly the right moment to make them ever more excited and dangerous. He eloquently counters what Brutus has said about Caesar being ambitious, reminding the plebeians that Caesar filled the Roman coffers with ransom money, showed compassion for the poor, and turned down the crown three times, all acts that did not suggest ambition. His speech is heavily laced with irony, as he repeats a statement that questions whether Brutus and the other assassins really are honorable men.

As Antony pauses to recover himself, the crowd characteristically begins to change sides again, now praising Antony rather than Brutus. Antony continues to criticize the *honorable men* and reveals that he has found Caesar's will, which benefits Romans greatly. Rather than read it immediately, he hints at the beneficial things it contains to reinforce how Caesar has been wronged and how much he loved his fellow citizens.

As the crowd becomes more and more stirred against the *honorable men*, Antony shows them Caesar's wounds, particularly emphasizing *the unkindest cut of all*, the one made by Brutus, and that broke the heart of Caesar.

Again demonstrating his ability to manipulate the crowd, Antony continues to say that he is not trying to stir them to riot, he does not wish to criticize the *honorable men,* and that he is a poor orator. ❂ How far do you agree with his assessment of himself?

Although he has previously said it would be better if the crowd did not hear the will because it demonstrates how much Caesar loved them, he now reminds them of it and reads it. The money and the parklands bequeathed to the people of Rome by Caesar in his will are enough to send the crowd off in a frenzy of revenge.

Antony, meanwhile, observes that the *Mischief* he has started is working. A servant comes to tell him that Octavius has reached Rome, and that Brutus and Cassius have fled.

STYLE AND LANGUAGE

Brutus and Antony show themselves to be eloquent and articulate individuals in this important scene. Brutus delivers his speech in the prose of informality as if among equals, whereas Antony's several speeches are in the formal verse appropriate to a state funeral. The first part of Antony's speech is almost poetry, as he repeatedly refers to Caesar's ambition and how the assassins are *honorable men.* Both men use rhetoric and obey the conventions of public speaking (see The Exam Essay, p. 75).

Act 3 *scene* 3

◆ The plebeians kill Cinna the poet.

♠ Cinna the poet, having dreamed that he *did feast with Caesar,* is drawn out of doors against his better judgment. The dream is a bad omen. Four plebeians question him and, in particular, want to know if he is going to Caesar's funeral as a friend or an enemy. Even though Cinna states that he goes as a friend, the plebeians, on hearing that his name is Cinna, tear him to pieces. Shakespeare makes sure that the audience knows that Antony's prediction of barbarous upheaval is coming true by making the plebeians leave the stage stating their intentions to go to the houses of the other conspirators.

Find the phrase

? What did Caesar leave to the Romans in his will (lines 255–265)?

? Find the lines said by plebeians in Act 2, scene 2 that show how quickly they change their minds about Brutus.

now take a break before the squabbling begins

Act 4 *scene* 1

◆ The relationship between the triumvirs is under stress.

The triumvirs (three people who jointly hold office), Antony, Octavius, and Lepidus, discuss assassinating anyone who may threaten their supremacy now that they jointly run Rome. Lepidus agrees to his brother's execution, and Antony has to agree to the death of Publius, his nephew.

To mark a contrast in Antony's attitude during Act 3, scene 2, when he outlines Caesar's generosity, he sends Lepidus off to get Caesar's will in the hope that they will find some way to cut costs to raise money for their armies. Antony criticizes Lepidus when he has left. When Octavius points out that Antony agreed to Lepidus becoming joint ruler, Antony puts him in his place by reminding him that he, Antony, is older than Octavius, the implication being that this also makes him wiser.

Octavius sticks up for Lepidus but Antony goes on to say that Lepidus will be useful only to share any blame leveled at them. He compares Lepidus to a horse, meaning that he is a resource to be used rather than taken notice of. Antony's final damning comment is: *Do not talk of him/ But as a property.*

The scene closes with Antony and Octavius agreeing to discuss tactics against Brutus and Cassius. It is becoming clear that the general unrest in Rome is also evident among the three new rulers who need to operate in harmony, but are privately disunited. A more ruthless side of Antony has been revealed.

Act 4 scene 2

◆ Brutus reveals displeasure with Cassius.
◆ Cassius is angry with Brutus.

BRUTUS REVEALS DISPLEASURE WITH CASSIUS (LINES 1–33)

The scene shifts to Sardis and, just as all is not well in Antony's camp, it is the same in that of Brutus. Brutus is greeted by Pindarus with the news that Cassius is on his way. He confides to Pindarus that he is displeased by some things that Cassius or his officers have done and he awaits an explanation.

Worried, Brutus asks his own officer, Lucilius, how Cassius greeted him. Confirming his suspicions, Brutus is told that Cassius's manner was unusually formal rather than friendly.

CASSIUS IS ANGRY WITH BRUTUS (LINES 34–58)

Cassius arrives and, in front of everyone, comes straight to the point: *Most noble brother, you have done me wrong.* They begin to discuss their differences, but Brutus tells Cassius to keep his voice down, saying that they must keep their disagreements private from their armies who should only see them united. Both men instruct their officers to lead their armies away from Brutus's tent and to let no one near until they have finished talking.

Act 4 scene 3

◆ Brutus and Cassius quarrel bitterly.
◆ The quarrel is resolved and their closeness restored.
◆ Brutus, Cassius, and generals discuss tactics.
◆ Brutus sees the ghost of Caesar.

Brutus and Cassius quarrel bitterly (lines 1–119)

In the privacy of Brutus's tent, the two allies argue. The specific matter that causes the quarrel is that Cassius has protected a corrupt officer, Lucius Pella, and Brutus has exposed it. Lucius Pella's crime has been to accept bribes from the Sardinians, and Cassius thinks it a small indiscretion that is understandable during such times of civil strife. Brutus points out that Cassius has compromised himself by supporting Lucius Pella, and adds that Cassius is himself too prone to bribery. He explains that they have killed Caesar for the sake of justice, and should demonstrate their own commitment to it at all levels. ✪ How far do you agree with him?

The angry Cassius rather weakly asserts that his greater age should enable him to be unquestioned in these matters, but Brutus scoffs at him and his lack of integrity. Cassius ironically comments that Caesar would not have dared to challenge him, and Brutus points out that Cassius would not have dared to have upset Caesar as he has Brutus. Cassius threatens Brutus, who is not afraid because he is convinced that he has right on his side. Brutus then reveals the reason for his displeasure with Cassius.

Cassius has apparently refused to send money to Brutus to finance his armies in their common interest, but Cassius plays this down, blaming the messenger for an inaccurate message. He also says that they should tolerate each other's faults.

Cassius then falls into a pit of self-pity, in which he moans that nobody likes him, life is not worth living, and he might as well offer Brutus his life as put up with his displeasure.

THE QUARREL IS RESOLVED AND THEIR CLOSENESS RESTORED (lines 120–187)

Cassius's self-pity seems to soften Brutus's attitude toward him. With a hint of the indulgence and affection found in friendship, Brutus observes that Cassius is too prone to losing his temper quickly and then relenting. The two make up as a poet forces an interview with them.

The poet is concerned that they should not be left alone because anything might happen if they quarrel. Cassius would indulge him but Brutus petulantly dismisses him for entering without permission.

♠ Reunited in friendship, Brutus confides to Cassius that he has *many griefs*. The only one he elaborates on is that Portia has committed suicide because of his absence and the gathering strength of Antony and Octavius.

BRUTUS, CASSIUS, AND GENERALS DISCUSS TACTICS (LINES 188–277)

The generals Titinius and Messala join Brutus and Cassius. At first they exchange information and then plan their campaign. Antony and Octavius apparently intend to attack them at Philippi with large armies, and, though they have different reports of how many, between 70 and 100 senators have been executed. Messala, believing he is the first to break the news, confirms Portia's death to Brutus. Knowing this already, he is able to "take it like a Roman" and move on to planning the campaign. It has also been suggested that Shakespeare forgot to remove one of the two reports of Portia's death, because Brutus would be unlikely to accept the false glory arising from his apparent fortitude.

Cassius believes the best tactic is to let the enemy come to them so that their own army will be fresher. Brutus disagrees because the ordinary people between Sardis and Philippi could easily be persuaded to join Antony, which would boost the attackers' morale and swell their numbers. Brutus forcefully refuses to listen further to Cassius's reasons, adding that it is important to seize their advantage of large numbers before their enemies enlarge theirs. They agree that they will march to Philippi instead of waiting, and disperse for the night.

BRUTUS SEES THE GHOST OF CAESAR (LINES 278–355)

Brutus is left alone and sends for two servants to sleep in his tent. He says this is because he may want to send them to Cassius on business in the night. ◐ What other reasons do you think he might have for not wishing to be left alone?

The gentle side of Brutus shows as he asks Lucius, his servant boy, to play a tune for him. As he sits awake and reads, unable to sleep, the ghost of Caesar appears and tells him it will meet him at Philippi. The ghost vanishes before Brutus plucks up courage to confront it. He wakes everyone up to ask if they cried out or saw anything, but no one did. ❂ How do you think you would feel if you saw the ghost of someone you had murdered? Do you think Brutus has any other reason for waking up the others?

STYLE AND LANGUAGE

Brutus says to Cassius: *You wronged yourself to write in such a case* (line 6). Although Brutus is referring to the letter Cassius has written on Lucius Pella's behalf, the word "write" is a play on words. It has a double meaning: write/right.

In Brutus's speech beginning *All this?* (line 46), he refers to Cassius's choleric temperament. This is a further mention of the ill health that is so often referred to in *Julius Caesar*. In the same speech, Brutus talks of *venom*, which echoes the snake imagery he used when convincing himself that Caesar must die (Act 2, scene 1, lines 10–36). Brutus again conjures up the imagery of the transformation of materials when he talks of Cassius's quick temper (lines 122–127).

The poet, a new character, seems to serve little purpose, but he does help to break up the tension that has been evident between Cassius and Brutus (lines 143–151). More important, his appearance echoes the incident in Act 3, scene 1 when Caesar ignores the warning letter from Artemidorus. Brutus dismisses the concerned and well-meaning poet with the words: *I'll know his humor, when he knows his time*, meaning that choosing the right time to say something is more important than what one actually has to say. By this echoing of Caesar's behavior, Shakespeare hints that Brutus may be doomed like Caesar.

Over to you

? Why does Brutus think it is important that he and Cassius discuss their differences in private rather than in front of their armies?

65

? When they quarrel, in Act 4, scene 3, who argues his case best – Brutus or Cassius? Which one has the moral upper hand?

? How real do you think Caesar's ghost is? Can you think of any other explanation for its appearance?

now take a break before preparing for battle

Act 5 *scene* 1

◆ The enemies talk and prepare for battle.

The Act opens with Octavius observing that the armies of Brutus and Cassius have unexpectedly come to Philippi rather than staying in the hills. Antony thinks his enemies are trying to give the impression of *fearful bravery*, when in reality they may be frightened.

Brutus and Cassius show all the signs of being ready for battle and enter the stage to talk with Antony and Octavius. Their conversation achieves little, however. Brutus and Cassius are not able to present convincing reasons for resolving anything, and Antony and Octavius are still angry. They are determined to avenge Caesar's death and regard Brutus and Cassius as traitors. Since the talks achieve little, both sides make preparations for battle.

We learn that it happens to be Cassius's birthday, a piece of information that carries with it the suggestion that it may also be his death day. This is reinforced by bad omens in the bird kingdom, observed by Cassius on his journey from Sardis to Philippi.

In contemplation of the day ahead and aware of the dangers that might befall them, Brutus and Cassius say their good-byes in case they do not live to meet again.

STYLE AND LANGUAGE

Note the use of animal imagery in this scene. Antony compares Brutus and Cassius to apes, hounds, and curs (lines 42–48). Cassius also informs us that two eagles, representing Antony and Octavius, have fed upon the armies of Brutus and Cassius and left birds of prey waiting to pick at their entrails.

Act 5 *scene* 2

◆ Brutus senses an advantage.

This short scene serves to suggest that at this point in the battle Brutus has the advantage over Octavius, whose soldiers seem to lack a fighting spirit. Brutus tells Messala to attack and capitalize on the opportunity.

Act 5 *scene* 3

◆ The advantage shifts to Antony and Octavius.
◆ Cassius and Titinius die.
◆ Brutus mourns and prepares to resume fighting.

THE ADVANTAGE SHIFTS TO ANTONY AND OCTAVIUS (LINES 1–34)

This scene demonstrates how errors and misinformation lead to the downfall of Cassius and Brutus. It begins with Cassius and Titinius in discussion. Cassius thinks his soldiers have become traitors and joined the enemy. Titinius thinks that Brutus attacked too early and suffered many casualties, and that his and Cassius's armies are surrounded by Antony's army.

The demoralized Cassius, Titinius, and Pindarus retreat to a hill where they can observe the battlefield. Cassius sends Titinius off to see whether his worst suspicions are correct. He also instructs Pindarus to watch what happens from higher up the hill because Pindarus has better eyesight. Now alone, Cassius ponders again the idea that his birthday may also be the day on which he dies.

Events take a serious turn as Pindarus reports that Titinius has been taken by the enemy, who shout for joy.

CASSIUS AND TITINIUS DIE (LINES 35–100)

Believing he is defeated, Cassius asks Pindarus, who owes him a favor, to kill him with the same sword he used to kill Caesar. His last words are addressed to the memory of Caesar avenged. Pindarus flees.

Cassius's fatal misinterpretation of events becomes apparent when Titinius returns with Messala. Brutus has defeated Octavius, and Antony has defeated Cassius. In reality, it has been Brutus's soldiers who greeted Titinius with joy – Pindarus has made a mistake. This news comes too late for Cassius who is already dead. As Messala goes to find Brutus, Titinius, overcome with grief for Cassius, kills himself.

BRUTUS MOURNS AND PREPARES TO RESUME FIGHTING (LINES 101–123)

 Brutus and several of his generals arrive on the scene knowing that Cassius is dead but unaware that Titinius is also dead. Just as Cassius remembered Caesar's power before he died, so Brutus says: *O Julius Caesar, thou art mighty yet!* He mourns the two soldiers as the last Romans of their caliber. He instructs his officers to remove Cassius's body to Thasos where the sight of it will be less likely to demoralize his troops. He then tells his generals to prepare for a second battle.

 STYLE AND LANGUAGE

Messala mixes the frequently used imagery of knives and venom to describe how the news of Cassius's death on Brutus will be like a poisoned dart piercing him.

Act 5 *scene* 4

◆ Lucilius pretends to be Brutus when captured.

This scene takes place during the battle. Cato, one of Brutus's soldiers, is killed and Lucilius is taken. He claims to be Brutus but Antony knows he is not. Lucilius says that Brutus, a true Roman, will not be taken alive. Displaying a more pleasant side of his character than we have seen for some time, Antony wants the imposter to be treated well and hopes for news of Brutus and the campaign.

Act 5 *scene* 5

◆ Brutus loses the battle and dies.
◆ Antony pays tribute to Brutus.

BRUTUS LOSES THE BATTLE AND DIES (LINES 1–57)

♠ Brutus and his *poor remains of friends* have lost the battle. Realizing this, Brutus asks first Clitus and then Dardanius to kill him, but they will not. Brutus tells his old school friend Volumnius that he knows his *hour is come* because during the previous night he has again seen the ghost of Caesar. Brutus reasons that: *It is more worthy to leap in ourselves/ Than tarry till they push us.* He asks his friend to kill him, but Volumnius also refuses.

As alarms sound increasingly often, Brutus says good-bye to his friends and rejoices that he will have more glory than Antony and Octavius. ✪ Why do you think he thinks this? Do you think he is right?

At last Brutus finds an accomplice in his suicide, Strato, who will hold Brutus's sword while its owner impales himself on it. Brutus, like Cassius, remembers Julius Caesar as he prepares to die – his last words, a **rhyming couplet** are: *Caesar, now be still/ I killed thee not with half so good a will.*

ANTONY PAYS TRIBUTE TO BRUTUS (LINES 58–87)

The play closes with the victors, Antony and Octavius, arriving with some of Brutus's men. Strato observes that Brutus has died an honorable death by not being taken captive. Octavius offers to take Strato into his own army, and Strato is willing if his commander Messala will release him. Because Strato has done a brave service to Brutus by helping him to kill himself, Messala releases him to the service of Octavius.

Antony closes the play by paying tribute to Brutus. He calls him *the noblest Roman of them all* because he was the only one of the conspirators who killed Caesar through an intention to do good rather than for personal gain and jealousy of Caesar's power. Just in the way that Brutus showed respect for Caesar as he died, so Antony commands that Brutus's body shall lie in state in his tent that night, and receive all the burial rites due to an honorable man.

Test yourself

? How many times was Caesar stabbed (Act 5, scene 1, line 56)?

? Where does Pindarus go after he has killed Cassius (lines 52–55)?

? Look at the summary list of key points below. Try to put them in the right order (answers at the bottom of the page):

A Relations in both leaderships strained.

B Brutus dies, Caesar is avenged.

C Antony makes crowd riot.

D Cassius makes mistake and dies.

E Caesar is murdered.

F Caesar ignores warning to *beware the ides of March*.

G Romans celebrate Caesar's victories.

H Cassius turns Brutus against Caesar.

I Brutus reluctantly joins conspirators.

J Caesar will not be warned.

TOPICS FOR DISCUSSION AND BRAINSTORMING

One of the best ways to review is with one or more friends. Even if you're with someone who hardly knows the text you're studying, you'll find that having to explain things to your friend will help you to organize your own thoughts and memorize key points. If you're with someone who has studied the text, you'll find that the things you can't remember are different from the things your friend can't remember, so you'll be able to help each other.

Discussion will also help you to develop interesting new ideas that perhaps neither of you would have had alone. Use a **brainstorming** approach to tackle any of the topics listed below. Allow yourself to share whatever ideas come into your head, however meaningless they seem. This will get you thinking creatively.

Whether alone or with a friend, use Mind Mapping (see p. vi) to help you brainstorm and organize your ideas. If you are with a friend, use a large sheet of paper and thick colored pens.

Any of the topics below could appear on an exam, but if you think you've found one in your actual exam, be sure to read the wording carefully and answer the precise question given.

TOPICS

Who's who?

1 Write a resumé for a character in the play who might be applying for a job in politics. Include age, interests, education, qualifications, achievements, and personal qualities.
2 Who are the Tribunes and what is their job?
3 What is a triumvirate and who are the triumvirs?
4 How do the plebeians contribute to the drama?
5 There are no real villains in *Julius Caesar*. Do you agree?
6 Which of the characters do you feel the most sympathy for? Why?
7 Which of the characters do you feel the least sympathy for? Why?

8 Which of the following adjectives describes one or more of the characters in *Julius Caesar*? Say which characters it descibes and find a line in the play to support your view for each.

conniving   devious   naïve   noble   brave
superstitious   nervous   domineering   honorable
ambitious   corrupt

9 Who were the following: Popilius Lena, Publius Cimber, and Lucius Pella?

Language

1 Write down the names of the main characters and leave plenty of space to write under the names. Now go through the play and list the animals used in reference to each character under their name.

2 What is dramatic irony? Give an example from the play.

3 As a public speaker, who is the more eloquent, Brutus or Antony? Give reasons for your answer.

4 Who said the following, and what does it mean? If you can't remember look up the lines.
The fault, dear Brutus, is not in our stars,/ But in ourselves, that we are underlings (Act 1, scene 2).
But 'tis a common proof,/ That lowliness is young ambition's ladder (Act 2, scene 1).
Cowards die many times before their deaths;/ The valiant never taste of death but once (Act 2, scene 2).
There is no fellow in the firmament (Act 3, scene 1).
When love begins to sicken and decay,/ It useth an enforced ceremony (Act 4, scene 2).

5 Add the next line to the following quotation:
Friends, Romans, countrymen, lend me your ears (Act 3, scene 2).

6 Add the next two lines to the following quotation and explain them in your own words:
There is a tide in the affairs of men,/ Which, taken at the flood, leads on to fortune (Act 4, scene 3).

7 What are the characteristics of Shakespearean verse?

8 What is an iambic foot?

9 Some words have been left out of Antony's speech as he looks down over the body of Brutus. If you can't remember the exact word, add one that means the same and maintains the iambic rhythm:

This was the _____ Roman of them all.
All the _____ save only he
Did that they did in _____ of great Caesar;
He only, in a general _____ thought
And common _____ to all, made one of them.
His life was _____, and the _____
So mixed in him, that _____ might stand up
And say to all the _____ 'This was a _____!'

Structure

1 If you were producing *Julius Caesar* for the stage and making a film, what would be the main differences in your treatment?
2 How is the weather used in this play?
3 Which part of the play do you find easiest to understand?
4 Which part is most difficult? What can you do to improve your understanding?
5 If you were presenting the play for the stage, where would you put the intermission, and why?

Themes and issues

1 What is the difference between a democracy and a dictatorship? Which characters support which type of government?
2 What can you tell about the status of women in Rome from the way Shakespeare presents Portia and Calphurnia?
3 Do you think Caesar's assassination would have taken place without the support of Brutus?
4 List any errors of judgment you can think of in the play. Describe one of them in detail.
5 Do you think Shakespeare believed in fate, free will, or both?
6 With which character or characters do you think Shakespeare's sympathies lie?

HOW TO GET AN "A" IN ENGLISH LITERATURE

In all your study, in coursework, and in exams, be aware of the following:

- **Characterization** – the characters and what we know about them (what they say and do, how the author describes them), their relationships, and how they develop.
- **Plot and structure** – what happens and how the plot is organized into parts or episodes.
- **Setting and atmosphere** – the changing scene and how it reflects the story (for example, a storm reflecting a character's emotional difficulties).
- **Style and language** – the author's choice of words, and literary devices such as imagery, and how these reflect the mood.
- **Viewpoint** – how the story is told (for example, through an imaginary narrator, or in the third person but through the eyes of one character – "She was furious – how dare he!").
- **Social and historical context** – influences on the author (see Background in this guide).

Develop your ability to:

- Relate **detail** to **broader content, meaning, and style.**
- Show understanding of the author's **intentions, technique, and meaning** (brief and appropriate comparisons with other works by the same author will earn credit).
- Give **personal response and interpretation,** backed up by **examples** and short **quotations.**
- **Evaluate** the author's achievement (how completely does the author succeed and why?).

now onto the exam itself and how to plan your essays

THE EXAM ESSAY

Planning

A literary essay of about 250 to 400 words on a theme from *Julius Caesar* will challenge your skills as an essay writer. It is worth taking some time to plan your essay carefully. An excellent way to do this is in the three stages below:

1 Make a **Mind Map** of your ideas on the theme suggested. Brainstorm and write down any ideas that pop into your head.
2 Taking ideas from your Mind Map, **organize** them into an outline choosing a logical sequence of information. Choose significant details and quotations to support your main thesis.
3 Be sure you have both a strong **opening paragraph,** stating your main idea and giving the title and author of the literary work you will be discussing, and a **conclusion** that sums up your main points

Writing and editing

Write your essay carefully, allowing at least five minutes at the end to check for errors of fact as well as for correct spelling, grammar, and punctuation.

REMEMBER!

Stick to the thesis you are trying to support and avoid unnecessary plot summary. Always support your ideas with relevant details and quotations from the text.

Model answer and plan

The next (and final) chapter consists of a model essay on a theme from *Julius Caesar* followed by a Mind Map and an essay plan used to write it. Use these to get an idea of how an essay about *Julius Caesar* might be organized and how to break up your information into a logical sequence of paragraphs.

Before reading the answer, you might do a plan of your own, then compare it with the example. The numbered points with comments at the end show why it's a good answer.

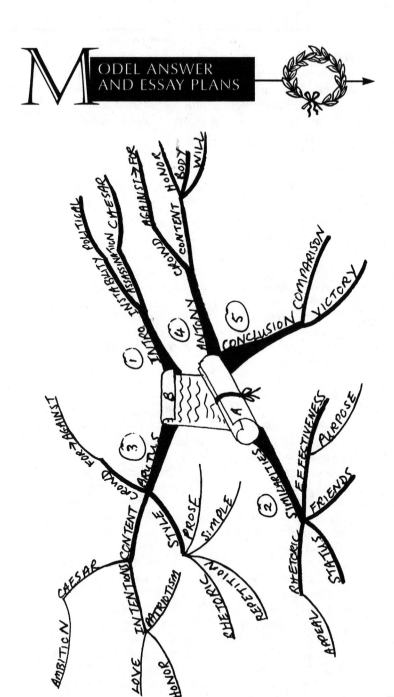

QUESTION — **In works of literature it is sometimes important for one character to try to influence the actions and ideas of other characters in the story. In Shakespeare's play *Julius Caesar,* both Brutus and Mark Antony try to influence the Roman people after Caesar's death. Discuss to what extent each is successful.**

PLAN

1 Introduction—Gives name and author of work to be discussed. States theme of essay and gives setting and context of Brutus's and Antony's speeches.

Body Paragraphs
2 Similarities between speeches, (rhetoric, effectiveness at public speaking), but differences, too.
3 Brutus's speech and what it says about him (crowd reaction, literary devices).
4 Antony's speech and what it says about him (crowd reaction, literary devices).
5 Conclusion — comparative eloquence/effectiveness. Antony wins.

ESSAY

The power of one character to influence others is often an important theme in literary works. This is particularly true in Shakespeare's play *Julius Caesar,* which is set in Ancient Rome. After the assassination of Julius Caesar, the most powerful leader Rome had ever known, the Roman people were left in danger of societal chaos. Brutus, formerly one of Caesar's closest friends but later one of his assassins, and Mark Antony, Caesar's second in command, vie with each other in their appeals to the Roman people for support.

Caesar's assassination, which occurs in the first scene of Act 2, threatens to plunge Rome into civil disorder, and it is of the utmost importance for Brutus and Antony to win the support of the populace. Both men have a similar status in Roman political life and both had formerly been Caesar's friend, but each has his own personal motives for his actions. Brutus, the democrat, believes that by killing Caesar he has acted in the common good, but Antony wants to avenge his beloved dictator and to advance himself. Both begin with the same sort of appeal for attention from a confused crowd. In their speeches, both men use the device of rhetoric – the art of asking questions to which they do not expect answers and that they supply themselves. Both men demonstrate their ability as statesmen. Beyond this there are mostly differences between the speeches.

Brutus's shorter speech comes first and relies heavily on the crowd having a good opinion of him. "Believe me for mine honor and have respect to mine honor." He presents the issue of why they killed Caesar democratically and with respect for the people. Brutus speaks in prose, perhaps because he is not as good an orator as Antony, but also because he wants to appeal to the common people. Brutus presents a series of contrasts saying, "Not that I loved Caesar less, but I loved Rome more." He wants the people to believe that he acted in their best interests to save them from a dictatorship, not because he hated Caesar but to save the people from Caesar's ambition. At this point the crowd is on his side.

Antony's speech, on the other hand, is much more clever and more manipulative. While, claiming, "I am no orator as Brutus is," he uses eloquent verse. He pretends to respect Brutus but zeroes in on the flaws in Brutus's arguments, telling the crowd that Caesar brought wealth to Rome, was kind to the poor, and rejected the crown three times. He plants the idea of "mutiny and rage" in the minds of the crowd, while claiming to do the opposite, and finally reads the crowd Caesar's will, so favorable to the people. Finally, Antony wins the people over to his point of view.

It is clear, therefore, that far from being "the plain blunt man" he claims to be, Antony is a skillful orator with the power to manage crowds. His speech is far more sophisticated than that of Brutus with its simple style and flawed argument. Shakespeare displays Antony's power to sway the fickle masses and with them over to his point of view. Thus, Antony is presented as a character whose words have an important impact on others and, in fact, have the power to change the course of Roman history.

WHAT'S SO GOOD ABOUT IT?

1 Strong introduction giving thesis, title, author, and setting of play.
2 Clear introduction of important characters.
3 Explains the importance of the two speeches.
4 Uses suitable quotations.

5 Shows understanding of Shakespeare's use of language.
6 Has well-organized and logical argument.
7 Uses correct standard English, spelling, and punctuation
8 Has strong conclusion proving thesis.

Some more themes to consider

QUESTION – How does Caesar get revenge?

PLAN

◆ Intro – although murdered, spirit lives on, drives rest of play.
◆ Antony's private speech marks turning point in play/swears revenge.
◆ Timely arrival of Octavius.
◆ Crowd manipulated by Antony.
◆ Brutus troubled by Caesar's ghost/illusion/error on battlefield.
◆ Cassius's mistake (remember quotes)/death.
◆ Conclusion – Brutus's death seals revenge.

QUESTION – Who is the hero in *Julius Caesar*?

PLAN

◆ Intro – no real heroes (Shakespearean tragedy/history plays).
◆ Why Caesar not hero (arrogant, ambitious, dictator).
◆ Why Brutus not hero (although for democracy, bad judgment about Caesar, lack of plan, naïve about human nature, mistake on battlefield).
◆ Cassius lacks heroic qualities.
◆ Antony not fully developed (Antony and Cleopatra) – instrument of Caesar's revenge.
◆ Conclusion – all characters too flawed to be heroes.

QUESTION – Compare and contrast Portia and Calphurnia

PLAN

◆ Intro – play about men, political/moral dilemmas, motives, judgment.

◆ Women had little role in such affairs in Rome (boy actors were used).
◆ Portia – assertive, concerned, sick with worry, can conceive of no life without Brutus, commits suicide. Husband respectful – treats her as equal.
◆ Calphurnia – begging, concerned, uncannily accurate intuition, treated as inferior by Caesar, disappears from play when she has no further purpose.
◆ Conclusion – both women presented with husbands in domestic context as caring wives (devices to show private lives of men and draw out their qualities). Fair reflection of actual role in Rome.

FURTHER QUESTIONS

Here are some more essay questions of the type you can expect to see on an exam. Try drawing a Mind Map for each one, then compare notes with a friend who has done the same.

1 Cassius says to Brutus: *Men at some time are masters of their fates* (Act 1, scene 2, line 146). How far does this statement apply to *Julius Caesar*?

2 The tragedy of Brutus lies in his inability to reconcile personal knowledge with political idealism. Do you agree?

3 What part does ritual play in *Julius Caesar*?

4 In your view, who is best suited to rule Rome after Caesar – Brutus, Cassius, Antony, or Octavius?

5 In *Julius Caesar,* there is tension created by the conflict between duty and friendship. Give examples of this conflict and discuss how the characters resolve it.

6 *Julius Caesar* could be described as a play about political intrigue. Do you agree?

7 In what ways do the characters of Brutus and Cassius differ? Show how these differences become obvious in a scene or part of a scene in which Brutus and Cassius are together.

8 . What part do superstition and the supernatural play in the dramatic development of *Julius Caesar*?

9 The entry of Antony's servant in Act 3, scene 1 has been called the turning point of the play. Do you agree? Explain why or why not.

10 Distinguish between the two wives who are portrayed in *Julius Caesar.* Which wife has the better relationship with her husband?

11 Portia describes herself as having "a man's mind but a woman's might." What problems does this cause for her and how does she deal with them?

12 How does Cassius persuade Brutus and Casca to join the conspiracy? What does it show about Cassius's motives and character?

GLOSSARY OF LITERARY TERMS

alliteration   repetition of a sound at the beginnings of words; for example, *ladies' lips.*

aside   a short speech spoken by one character, as if thinking aloud, not meant to be heard by others onstage.

blank verse   the kind of nonrhyming verse in which Shakespeare usually writes, with five pairs of syllables to each line, with the stress always on the second syllable; unrhymed iambic pentameter (see p. 37).

context   the social and historical influences on the author.

couplet   *see* rhyming couplet.

dramatic irony   *see* **irony (dramatic).**

foreshadowing   an indirect warning of things to come, often through imagery.

iambic pentameter   verse with five pairs of syllables to a line, with the stress always on the second syllable.

image   a word picture used to make an idea come alive, as a **metaphor**, **simile**, or **personification** (see separate entries).

imagery   the kind of word picture used to make an idea come alive.

irony   **(dramatic)** where at least one character onstage is unaware of an important fact that the audience knows about, and that is somehow hinted at; **(simple)** when the opposite of what is meant is said, or when something turns out in the opposite way to that which is intended (see p. 39).

metaphor   a description of a thing as if it were something essentially different but also in some way similar; for example, *the word of Caesar might/ have stood against the world* (like one soldier).

meter   a form of poetic rhythm determined by the number and length of feet in a line.

metrical foot   a number of syllables making up one beat in a verse style's meter.

personification   a description of something as if it were a person; for example, *His coward lips did from their colour fly.*

prose   language in which, unlike verse, there is no set number of syllables in a line, and no rhyming (see p. 36).

pun   a use of a word with two meanings, or of two similar-sounding words, where both meanings are appropriate in different ways (see p. 45).

rhetoric   the art of effective or persuasive speaking or writing in which the speaker asks questions without expecting them to be answered (see p. 40).

rhyming couplet   a pair of rhyming lines, often used at the end of a speech.

setting   the place in which the action occurs, usually affecting the atmosphere; for example, the battlefield.

simile   a comparison of two things that are different in most ways but similar in one important way; for example, *he doth bestride the narrow world/ Like a Collossus.*

soliloquy   a speech spoken by an actor alone onstage as if thinking aloud.

structure   how the plot is organized.

theme   an idea explored by an author; fate and free will, for example.

tragedy   a play focusing on a tragic hero (see separate entry) or couple.

tragic hero   a character whose nobility or achievement we admire, and whose downfall and death through a weakness or error, coupled with fate, arouses our sympathy.

viewpoint   how the story is told – through action, or in discussion between minor characters, for instance.

NDEX